KT-472-595

CHILDREN OF THE SUN

Morris West was born in Australia, where he served a six-year novitiate with the Christian Brothers but left before taking his final vows. He became a teacher and joined the army in 1940. After the war he moved to Europe, where he now lives with his family, and began writing: his fourteen books have been translated into twenty-seven languages. *The Devil's Advocate*, one of the most famous, is now a major film, and cinema versions of other novels including *Harlequin* are planned. His most recent novel is *The Navigator*, published by William Collins in 1976.

Morris West has always been renowned for the authenticity of his facts and settings, whether connected with diplomacy, religion, international business or science, and each of his books was written after extensive travel and research in countries throughout the world

Available in Fontana by the same author

The Devil's Advocate
Daughter of Silence
The Big Story
The Shoes of the Fisherman
Harlequin

MORRIS WEST

Children of the Sun

FONTANA BOOKS
by agreement with
HEINEMANN

First published in Great Britain in 1957
by William Heinemann Ltd
First published in Fontana Books 1977

All rights reserved

Made and printed in Great Britain by
William Collins Sons and Co Ltd Glasgow

For
ALISON DIX GARGIULO

CONDITIONS OF SALE
This book is sold subject to the condition that
it shall not, by way of trade or otherwise, be lent,
re-sold, hired out or otherwise circulated without
the publisher's prior consent in any form of
binding or cover other than that in which it is
published and without a similar condition
including this condition being imposed on the
subsequent purchaser

CONTENTS

ACKNOWLEDGEMENT

To name some, without naming all, would be
an injustice. Many honest and enlightened men
and women who helped me with this book have
asked me to suppress their names for fear of
economic reprisals against themselves and their
families. I offer them, nameless, my thanks for
their help and for the privilege of
their friendship.
M.L.W.

ILLUSTRATIONS
(*between pages* 96 *and* 97)

Souls made of fire, children of the sun,
With whom revenge is virtue.

The Revenge, Act V., Sc. 2
EDWARD YOUNG (1684–1765)

PROLOGUE

IN NAPLES the nightmares began. They began, as they always do, with a simple reality.

There was a child whom I used to visit in the House of the Urchins. His name was Antonino. He was eight years old, but his body was so small and his face so pinched and pale that you would have taken him for five or six. When I came into the small and dusty courtyard where he played with the other boys, he would leave the game immediately and run to me, arms outstretched, calling my name, "Signor Mauro! Signor Mauro!"

When I took him in my arms, he would cling to me a while, then he would beg me to sit down and tell him stories of my country—how far it was from Naples, and what sort of people lived there, and what language they spoke and what birds were there and what animals.

While we were talking the others would gather around, and I would find myself the centre of a group of boys, open-mouthed, spellbound, as if they were watching Punchinello in his little golden house with the red curtains. Whenever a new one joined us, Antonino would introduce him to me and tell him with grave face and wide gestures that I was a "*gran' scrittore australiano*" who came from a country bigger than Europe where no one, no one at all, was hungry.

When I got up to leave, he would hold my hand and trot beside me on his rickety little legs and beg to carry my coat or my camera, so that he could be with me a few minutes longer. When I walked down the narrow street, between the fish stalls and the piles of refuse and the drab lines of laundry, I would look back and wave, and he would wave too, and my heart would be wrenched with pity and with tenderness and with deep, deep shame.

For Antonino was a *scugnizzo*, a homeless, loveless child of the back alleys of Naples.

He didn't belong to Naples; he came from Rome. He had made the journey alone, on foot, sleeping in ditches, scavenging like an animal for food, his feet bare, his clothes a mess of filthy rags. When he reached the outskirts of the city, he had made a frightening journey through the mazes of the underground railway, and had come finally to rest on an iron grating in the Street of the Two Lepers. He had joined a gang of other waifs who lived by scavenging and pilfering and pimping for the girls in the *casino*.

Each night he slept on a grating where the warm air drifted up from the baker's oven, or between the wheels of a vendor's cart or on the stone steps of an ancient church. Until one night he was picked up and brought to the House of the Urchins.

He was safe there and warm and loved, more than he had ever been loved in his life. His frail body began to strengthen and his tormented little mind began to calm itself. But he would never be a child again, and when he became a man he would always be different from other men, because the scar of the streets was on him and the fear of the sunless days and the terror of the loveless nights.

In the House of the Urchins they would try to make him forget. But he would never forget, because, one day, he must grow up and go out again into the old and pitiless city.

So, I began to dream about him. . . .

Always the dream was the same. It was night, a moonlit night, chill and dreary. There was a railroad track—a long

perspective of steel rails between tall poplars, naked and
skeletal as they are in winter. At the end of the track, where
the lines converged, there was a tunnel, a black archway in
a grey cliff.

There was a child walking along the rails, a ragged,
spindly, limping child. Sometimes he would stumble and
fall, then pick himself up and limp forward again. My heart
went out to him with love and pity, but, when I called to
him, he began to run.

I followed him, calling all the time, begging him to stop,
warning him of the dangers that lurked in the dark tunnel.
Still he went on. The dark archway swallowed him up. I
followed. There were lights in the tunnel, rare, yellow
lights and against them I saw his tiny distorted body, hop-
ping like a wounded animal from sleeper to sleeper.

I heard the sound of a locomotive. I shouted to warn
him, but he would not stop. He was running to his death
but he did not seem to care. Then I saw the headlamp of
the locomotive, and, in its light, the face of the child—not
Antonino's face, but the face of my own son!

Always at this same moment I would wake, sweating and
terrified and calling the name of my child who was sleeping
quietly in his bed, smiling at his own untroubled dreams.

Then I knew that I must write this book, to purge myself of the nightmare. I must make my voice the voice of
the children, the hungry, the homeless, the dispossessed,
the damned innocents of Naples. I must batter on hearts
for them, scavenging as they scavenge, not for bread, but
for pity and for human kindness and above all for hope.

PART ONE

'SEE NAPLES AND DIE'

CHAPTER ONE

THERE IS a street in Naples called the Street of the Two
Lepers.

To find it you must plunge into the labyrinth of lanes
and alleys on the north side of the Via Roma. You must
thread your way through steep, narrow ravines of houses,
with lines of washing hung between them like the banners
of a tatterdemalion triumph. You push through the crowds
round the fruit stalls and the fish barrows with their mountains of mussels and trays of polypi and their tubs of slimy
water crawling with snails. You brush by the hawkers with
their piles of cheap cottons and second-hand jackets and
patched trousers and their photographs of film stars in
cheap gilt frames. You duck under the cheeses and sausages
hanging from the windows of the *salumeria*; you stumble
over the grubby tattered children rooting in the rubbish
piles for rinds and fruit scraps and trodden cigarette butts.
You pass a dozen shrines with dusty statues or pictures of
gaudy saints behind smeared and spotted glass. The lamps
glow dully and the little votive tapers flutter faintly in the
chill stirring of the wind. You peer into tiny rooms where
women with pinched faces bend over knitting or embroid-
ery, or where families of ten and twelve chatter and gesticu-
late over bowls of steaming *pasta*.

Finally, you come to the Street of the Two Lepers.

There is no commerce here. It is a dark and narrow lane,

whose walls are damp and slimy and whose doors are blind arches, cold and cheerless. Yet, as you pass, you see that they are astir with life. Shapeless figures sit huddled over tin dishes filled with warm charcoal ash. A bundle of rags groans and stretches out a hand in supplication. In a gloomy courtyard, where a dull lamp burns in a tiny niche, a troop of filthy children link hands and dance in a pitiful mockery of joy. The cold bites into you and you thrust your hands deeper into your pockets, duck your head under the arch of a Spanish buttress and plunge onward towards the light at the far end of the Street of the Two Lepers.

When you reach it, you find yourself in a small square with a pile of rubble in the centre and a small traffic of people, grey-faced and shabby, passing and repassing from the dark lanes into the yellow light of the square and the streets of the vendors.

It was in this square that Peppino gave me my first lesson on Naples.

For me, it was an important occasion. I had dressed for it with some care. I wore an old seaman's jersey, frayed and darned in many places. My trousers were tattered and patched and I wore a pair of broken shoes with pointed toes that hurt my feet abominably. I had not shaved for three days and my nails were black and my hands were stained with grease and tobacco tar. In any other city I would have been moved on by the police, but here, in the *bassi* of Naples, I was dressed like a thousand others.

Even so, it was difficult to escape attention. I am a big man, six feet tall with broad shoulders and big hands and big feet. My hair is brown and my eyes are light hazel, and when Peppino walked beside me we looked like David and Goliath.

I needed Peppino. I needed him to vouch for me as a friend and a good fellow who knew how to keep his mouth shut. I needed his reassurance in the labyrinthine darkness of the Neapolitan ant-heap. I needed him to interpret for me the strange Neapolitan dialect—an esoteric tongue which only the initiate can understand. I speak fair Tuscan and am comfortable enough with polite people, but here, without Peppino, I might have been deaf and dumb.

To tell you at this point the full story of Peppino himself would be not only to anticipate, but to make a mystery for you, a mystery you might be inclined to dismiss as an improbable lie. Let it suffice for now that Peppino is a Neapolitan, that he is twenty years of age, that he was once a scugnizzo, an urchin who lived in the streets as thousands of others live today, that he has been in a house of correction and that now, by a singular and miraculous mercy, he is a man who respects himself and is respected by others.

He was recommended to me as one who could show me the life of Naples, teach me to understand it, and help me to explain it to the rest of the world, who live so remote from misery that they can neither understand nor succour it.

* * *

It was nine in the evening. We sat, Peppino and I, on the heap of rubble in the centre of the square, smoking cigarettes and watching the passage of the people.

In front of us was a door. Unlike the other doorways in the square and in the lanes, this one was brightly lit with a neon tube and an illuminated number. A man stood leaning against the door jamb. He was short, stocky and well-dressed, with sleek black hair and a flashing smile and dead, dark eyes in a Levantine face.

When a man or a group of youths came to the door, he would give them a quick appraising glance, then move aside to let them go in. When anyone came out, he would glance over his shoulder as if waiting for a sign of approval before letting them leave the premises. All the time, he never said a word.

"That," said Peppino, "is a casino—a closed house. The man is the keeper of the women."

I nodded. So much was evident. A brothel looks the same in all languages, and so do the men who run them.

I was more interested in the steady stream of youths and men who came and went under the naked neon tube. One is apt to be deceived by the look of these small and under-nourished people, but I was certain some of the lads were no more than sixteen years of age. I put the question to Peppino. He shrugged and spread his hand and cocked his head on one side in the peculiar deprecating gesture of the Neapolitan.

"What do you expect, Mauro? In the city of Naples there are two hundred thousand men without work. Many of the lucky ones earn like me only five hundred lire a day. We have no hope of marriage. Who can keep a wife and children on six English shillings a day? We cannot have the company of a good girl without making her our *fidanzata*. And what father will promise his daughter to a man who cannot support her? What is left to us? This . . ." he flicked his cigarette ash in the direction of the casino, ". . . or five minutes in a dark corner with one of the girls of the street. *Capisce?*"

I shivered as though someone had walked over my grave.

I understood. I understood very well. Continence in expectation of marriage is one thing—good morals and good social practice. But continence without hope of marriage is a bleak sanctity attainable by few, and certainly not by these warm-blooded people of midday Italy, who sleep ten in a bed because they can't find more room to sleep in and couldn't pay for it if they did.

15

I understood something else, too—a thing that had puzzled me for a long time. As you walk the back streets of Naples you are conscious of the absence of women in the long lines of youths and men making the *passeggiata*, the evening walk, clustered round a shop window, lounging around the bars, singing, laughing, shouting, quarrelling amiably about the latest sporting results. When you ask for an explanation, they tell you, with pride, that the place for a good girl is in the house with her family, or with her fidanzato. If she goes out with a man she is a bad girl by presumption and generally in fact. The concept of friendship between the sexes is alien to these people.

"Friendship goes quickly to the act," as Peppino told me succinctly. "The only safety for a good girl is to stay at home and wait for a good husband."

"And if she can't get a husband?"

Peppino shrugged.

"That is why it is so hard to find a good girl. If I wished to get married, which I cannot do, I should take a long time and search carefully before I could be sure." He broke off, tugged at my sleeve and slewed me round to look at the opposite side of the square. "Look, Mauro! This is another thing you must see."

The wall of the little piazza was broken by a narrow lane, at the mouth of which stood a trio of American sailors on shore leave from the aircraft carrier anchored in the bay. They were young, tall, blond and good humoured, and if they were drunk they showed no signs of it. One of them carried brown paper parcels and the other two had small cameras slung around their necks.

Around them danced three small boys who looked only five or six but were probably nearer to ten. Their voices were shrill and piping and they carried clearly across the tiny space. In a mixture of dockside English, Neapolitan

16

and Italian, they were crying the charms of the girls in the casino. Their gestures were the timeless obscenities of the trade and the words they used sounded a blasphemy from their childish lips. The three sailor-boys laughed uneasily and looked at each other. They were young and a little scared but curious and interested in the old proposition. They stood irresolutely for a moment, then tried to move away.

The boys danced round them and shouted more loudly. They were like dogs herding unruly sheep. Their performance was as cunning as if it had been scored for them. Dancing, piping, tugging at sleeves and arms, they edged the sailors slowly round the square until they stood almost opposite the door of the casino.

Then, as they stood undecided, the Levantine took over. He smiled and pointed inside and made what seemed to be an encouraging speech in English. Two minutes later the boys filed through under the neon light and were lost to view. Only the urchins were left and the sleek-haired Levantine. They talked quietly, with gestures that indicated a financial calculation; then the boys moved away, apparently satisfied, while the Levantine leaned against the door jamb and picked his teeth with a match.

I reached for a cigarette. When I came to light it, my hands were trembling. The performance had sickened me. I wanted to leave the place for ever and go back to my own country where the air was clean and the children were sleeping in their beds untouched by the dirt of the old world.

Peppino looked at me. His dark eyes were sombre.

"Did it please you, Mauro?"

"It made me sick."

He shrugged.

"I used to do that once, Mauro. Every night. Sometimes I used to sell the sailors to another who would bring them here. Sometimes I would sell them to older men who would rob them and steal their cameras and their clothes. It paid well. Tomorrow..." He pointed at the lighted doorway. "Tomorrow the children will come back and they will be paid a percentage of the price the sailors paid to the house. They will not be cheated. There is a *fiducia* —trust—between them."

"The trust of the gutter."

Peppino nodded soberly. His voice was sad and gentle.

"Sure, Mauro! Sure! The trust of the gutter. Except that here, in the bassi, we have no gutters. The filth runs down the centre of the streets where the children play. How can they fail to be touched by it? You asked me to show you this city. I tell you now, you have not yet begun to see it or to understand it. Before you judge us—any of us—wait! Wait and see!"

I looked up at him and saw that his eyes were wet with tears and his face was twisted with all the miseries he himself had endured before a hand reached out and plucked him out of the filth into a semblance of security. I was ashamed of my outburst. I reached out and put my hand on his shoulder. I said:

"Forgive me, Peppino. I'll wait. I'll try to understand."

He stood up and drew his jacket tighter about his thin shoulders.

"Come then, Mauro. Come and I will show you."

* * *

It was late and I was hungry. I had eaten breakfast and a midday lunch of fruit and fish, but now the night was half gone and I was irritable and faint with hunger. I suggested to Peppino that we turn into one of the kitchens and eat before we continued our promenade. He brushed the suggestion aside with a curt "Later! Later!" I knew that he had done twelve hours work on a cup of coffee and a hunk of dry bread, so I was ashamed to press the point and I followed him deeper and deeper into the maze of alleys behind the Via Roma.

They were paved with rough stone blocks, slippery with mud and foul with slops from the tenements. Refuse was piled in little heaps outside the doors and in the reeking angles behind the arches. Scraggy brown cats padded silently from one heap to the other and spat at us as we passed.

The blank walls hemmed us in and when I looked up I could see the black ribs of the balconies and the filter of light through the closed shutters. Far above us I could see a thin strip of sky and the twinkle of a few cold stars. High on the leprous walls were the outlines of ancient escutcheons, pitted and cracked and defaced, and here and there the shape of ancient wreaths and cherubs in broken stucco. I remembered that not one of these buildings was less than a hundred years old and that some of them dated back to the time of the Spaniards.

In the shadow of a crumbling arch Peppino stopped and drew me back into the shadows. We lit cigarettes and stood smoking them furtively, talking in low tones.

Across the alley were three doorways. They were open, in spite of the cold, and yellow bulbs were burning so that we could see inside the rooms. The first was a small cobbler's shop where a man and his two sons were working over their lasts, while a woman with a blonde girl on her lap sat talking to them. Behind them I caught a glimpse of another smaller room with a brass bedstead and a votive lamp burning in front of a coloured plaster statue of the Madonna.

The next door opened into a dwelling. There was a

very old woman, grey, gap-toothed and shapeless under a huddle of shawls, a middle-aged couple and six children, boys and girls, whose ages ranged from five to about eighteen. Nine people in all! They sat round a table eating the evening meal. The rest of the room was cluttered with a huge matrimonial bed, a sideboard and a large wardrobe, with a tiny Agipigas stove over which was hung an array of cooking vessels.

The third door opened into a narrow room with two single beds and a tiny table at which a mother and three teenage daughters were working on what looked like a wedding gown of white net. They had the grey, pinched look of people who work too long and eat too little and see too little sunlight.

"These," said Peppino, quietly, "these are the lucky ones. They have work to do and a house to live in. They are seldom hungry and their children are cared for."

I looked out at the festering alley and back again at the pitiful crowded rooms where these fortunate folk lived and worked their sweatshop hours. I looked at Peppino, wondering if he were laughing at me. He was quite serious.

"I show you this so that you will not think all of Naples is bad and hopeless. These are good people and they do not live badly. If only there were more like them, we should not be as unhappy as we are now."

"Nine people in a room? Where do they sleep?"

"In the bed. It is big, as you see."

"All of them?"

"Where else?"

"Is that good? The old, the young, men and women, the married, the unmarried, all in one bed?"

"No, it is not good. But it is better than the *baracche*—the shacks—where they sleep fifteen in a room. It is better than the ruins where there is no light, no warmth, nothing, and they sleep on the floor like animals. It is a thousand times better than the street, where the scugnizzi sleep, in the doorways and over the gratings and under the fruit barrows. Believe me, it is much, much better."

I believed him. Put that way, even a child could see it.

Misery is a relative word. If you have work in a city where there are two hundred thousand workless, you are fortunate indeed. If nine of you sleep in a bed instead of on a cold stone floor, then you should thank God for the mercy of it. If your children come home at night to eat and rest instead of scrabbling with the cats and sleeping on the baker's grating, then you are a lucky parent.

Privacy and ventilation and a bath and running water and a tub to wash your clothes in—these are unbelievable luxuries not to be thought on without presumption.

I remembered my pleasant villa at Sorrento, which has three bedrooms and two bathrooms and a room for the maid, who earns as much as the father of six children. I thought of the tourists who come to Naples and Pompeii and Amalfi and Capri, who sleep at the Excelsior and eat at Le Lucciole. I was ashamed and I was afraid.

Peppino was still waiting for me to speak. I asked him:

"Peppino, why do Neapolitans have such big families?"

He looked at me in surprise, then stuck out his chest with simple pride.

"Why not, Mauro? We are a people with warm blood. Our women are good breeders. We like children. Why should we not have them?"

It was too early in our acquaintance to press this point. I was interested in another line of thought.

"This man here." I pointed across to the family of six. "All these are his children?"

"Of course. All made in the same bed. He is a brave one that."

I was prepared to believe he was brave, though not in the Neapolitan sense. I said:

"But is it good, Peppino, that the act of love should be made here where the children can see it, and the young girls and their brothers who are growing up and feeling that they too are ready to be men and women?"

Peppino frowned. He flicked his cigarette butt on the ground and stamped on it. Then he turned to me.

"No, Mauro, it is not good. But that is the way it happens because we have no houses and no room and people must live this way or perish on the streets. The young ones know too early—and the ones who are ready sometimes do what should not be done with their own brothers or sisters. Often that is what drives them on to the streets, girls and boys. That is what prepares them for the streets—for things like you saw at the casino tonight. But how do you change it? We are a poor people. We have no work to do and no place to go to find it. *Cosa fare?* What's to do about it?"

Cosa fare?

I didn't know. I was tired and hungry and my feet were aching in the broken shoes. I wanted to be quit of the whole business. I wanted to forget this ancient misery of the people of Naples and go home to my own country or back to the bright islands where the tourists came and laughed and drank and tousled the well-fed girls.

I trod my cigarette into the mud and stepped out into the alley.

"Come on, Peppino. Let's eat!"

*   *   *

We would eat, said Peppino, in the Piazza Mercato. There was a kitchen there where the food was cheap and the wine was good and the proprietor was a friend of his.

The Piazza Mercato is at the far end of the city, just off the Strada della Marina. The most direct route from where we were was to cross the Via Roma, walk down the Via Sanfelice and work our way to the southern end of the Corso Umberto. But this did not suit Peppino's book at all. There were things to show me on the way; besides, we needed cigarettes.

I was prepared to suffer a necessary minimum of discomfort on this back-street pilgrimage, but I still clung stubbornly to the luxury of English cigarettes. The cheapest place to buy them was from the smugglers. Tobacco is a state monopoly in Italy and the range of products is poor. Besides, Italian cigarettes have a habit of coming apart at the seams before they are half smoked. So, to the smugglers we would go, the police and private conscience notwithstanding.

We crossed the Via Roma with its bright lights and screaming traffic and its well-dressed men and women making the ritual passeggiata, gaping at the shop windows, chatting in little groups, drinking tiny cups of espresso coffee in the bars where the windows were full of brightly-coloured Easter eggs. I was acutely aware of my shabby clothes and my grubby hands and my unshaven face, but no one took the slightest notice of me, and for once I was spared the attentions of the beggars and pedlars of sunglasses and picture postcards.

In a few moments we were back in the familiar setting of dark alleys and towering tenements and wineshops where shabby men sat among the barrels and the baskets and drank sparingly of the rich, raw wine. A litre of common wine costs 150 lire, and if you're earning only 500 a day you drink sparingly and smoke little. If you're single and free of family responsibilities you do a little better, but if you're a family man you can't afford the minor vices.

It was another sidelight on the self-evident problem of an impoverished land with a staggering birthrate.

The need for catharsis, for the periodic purging of grief and pain and fear is fundamental to human nature. In lands more prosperous and more evolved there are twenty ways in which a man may divert himself and forget the daily crucifixions of living. But here, in the bassi of Naples, there are only two—the commerce of the bed, and the rituals of the Church. The *letto di matrimonio* is as characteristic of Neapolitan life as the baroque churches with their dusty saints and their grotesque arrays of votive offerings, which puzzle even Catholics from other parts of the world.

I was still chewing the cud of this problem when Peppino drew me aside from the main concourse into a narrow lane and towards a small gathering of men and women sitting on cane-bottomed chairs outside the tenement doors.

"*Contrabbandieri,*" said Peppino, cheerfully. "Cigarettes!"

The first of the illicit vendors was a youngish matron with a tired face and sad eyes. Beside her squatted a tiny girl shivering in a thin cotton frock. Peppino walked up to her and pointed to the little tray she held in her lap. I saw a dozen packets of American cigarettes, all well-known brands. None of them carried the impost seal of the Italian Government. Peppino pointed again to the tray.

"*Americane. Ti piace?*"

I said they didn't please me. I have no taste for American cigarettes. I prefer the light yellow Virginia of the British makers.

Peppino asked her if she carried any English. She shook her head indifferently and jerked a thumb over her shoulder.

"*Giu*—further down."

We walked on to the next pedlars. They were a pair, a

24

man and a woman, and the trays they carried were bigger and better filled. She was a large and shapeless matron on the wrong side of fifty. Over her dirty black dress she wore three tattered pullovers, each of a different colour. The man was a small, wax-faced fellow with a turned eye. They looked up as we approached and exchanged suspicious glances. Once again my height and my complexion had betrayed me as a foreigner.

"English cigarettes?" enquired Peppino.

The woman nodded down at the tray but did not speak. I saw half a dozen good English brands, all with the cellophane seals intact. I chose two packets.

"How much?" asked Peppino.

"Two-fifty each."

It was a hundred lire below the regular market price for twenty cigarettes. Peppino nodded approval and I paid over 500 lire.

"Who is he?"

The man jerked his thumb at me, although one eye seemed to be peering away in the opposite direction.

"*Trentino*," said Peppino, curtly. "In trouble with the police."

This was a fiction we had agreed upon to explain my appearance and my taciturnity and my presence in the bassi of Naples.

The man nodded approvingly. This was something he could understand. Then an idea seemed to strike him. He thrust his hand into his pocket and brought out a small packet. When he opened it I saw that it contained three rubber contraceptives, each in a plastic container.

He offered them to me, but Peppino waved them aside curtly. I stepped forward and intercepted the gesture. I had reasons of my own for being interested in the proposition.

"How much?" I asked. "How much for each one?"

"Fifty lire."

"Each one?"

"Each one. A hundred and fifty the three."

I shook my head. He shrugged and thrust the packet back into his pocket. The price was his best offer. There was no room for bargaining. That gesture interested me, too. It gave me the statistic I wanted. But the trade wasn't finished yet. He had other wares to offer.

"Do you want a good girl? Clean, knowledgeable?"

"Where?"

"The girl?"

"Yes."

He gestured towards the far end of the street.

"Down there. I have only to call her and she will come."

"Where would we go?"

This time the gesture was over his shoulder, towards the open doorway of the room at his back. I looked in and saw the usual clutter of furniture, the huge bed and the lamp burning in front of a crude oleo of Saint Gennaro. I asked him:

"Whose?"

He looked puzzled.

"The girl?"

"No, the room."

His face brightened again.

"The room is ours. You can have it for an hour, two hours, as long as you like. It is clean and private."

Once again I told him no. Once again he shrugged and bent over his tray. The commerce was over. There was nothing more to talk about. Peppino and I turned away and headed southward towards the Piazza Mercato.

As we walked, Peppino talked about the smugglers and

how they came by their wares. He had worked for them once and his information was accurate. The cigarettes came from the ships, he said. They were thrown overboard in rubber bags and picked up by fishermen who brought them into harbour where the contact men picked them up and carried them to storehouses in the back streets. Sometimes the dockside officials were bribed to turn a blind eye to seamen who came ashore with bulging kitbags. The vendors were simply percentage salesmen who distributed the packages.

Didn't the police know about the trade? *Sicuro!* The police knew about it, but so long as it was confined to this back-street peddling they were prepared to let it flourish. Now and again they made a big strike at one of the major traffickers, but the police after all were Neapolitans and they, too, understood that people must live. And if there is no margin in the law for earning a crust of bread, then the administrators of the law must provide the leeway themselves.

I nodded and grunted and let the subject drop. I was busy with other thoughts and I was still not sure enough of Peppino to trust them to him. Later, when I came to know him better, when I myself was calmer and more dispassionate, we were able to talk freely, without rancour. At this moment, we were new to each other and I was tired and of uncertain temper.

*   *   *

Our brief contact with the cigarette salesman had brought me face to face with two facts that plagued me constantly during my investigations in Naples. First was the incredible venality of the Italians of the Mezzogiorno.

You see it at its lowest level in the back-street commerce of sex and contraband. Every tourist is affronted by it when his guide offers—for a consideration—to have the ladies shown the forbidden pornography of Pompeii, or when the attendants in the Naples Museum shuffle him into a quiet corner to take flash photographs of works of art.

It follows you down the Sorrentine Peninsula where the tourist shops charge double prices for intarsio work made at sweatshop rates in the back alleys. The simplest transaction, like letting a holiday villa, involves kick-backs and false declarations so that the owner doesn't have to pay taxes on the tenancy. For this reason one may find oneself, with some surprise, listed as a relative of one of the major families in the district. What the family saves on the deal I don't know, but there is no diminution of rent or in the cost of living.

On the upper levels of politics, diplomacy and finance, this venality flourishes like a rank growth poisoning the land, making it fruitless of reform or honest dealing. I was to learn more, much more about this as the days went on: payments for good marks at competitive examinations, payment for promotion, diversion of foreign aid to private pockets, all the shoddy machinations that keep the people of southern Italy in a state of marginal existence without hope of betterment.

Poverty is at the root of it. Poverty and the fear that springs from poverty, and the long history of oppression and speculation by the conquerors.

The servant is corrupted by the corruption of the masters —and the Spaniards and the Bourbons and the Allied armies were no paragons of social virtue. Neither are the men who rule Italy today. The people of the bassi live so close to hunger and death that they cannot spare a thought for the morals of an act that puts bread in their mouths.

The second fact, the ever-present fact, was the staggeringly high birthrate of Southern Italy. The city of Naples

28

crawls with children, from bare-bottomed infants to youths of eighteen.

The reasons for it are many: natural fertility, over-crowding, unemployment, lack of work, ignorance, the reactionary attitude of the southern clergy who refuse to preach the authorised version of birth-control by periodic abstinence.

The remedies are not as simple as they seem to the theorist living in a highly evolved country with full employment for both sexes.

In the breadline statistics of the bassi, a contraceptive costs the same as half a loaf of bread. Female appliances and solutions are correspondingly higher—even if there were doctors to advise on their use. In the Mezzogiorno there are none such—as I was to find out later. More than this, even the simplest methods require a minimum of privacy for their application. When you sleep ten in a bed, without bathroom or toilet, the situation becomes impossible.

The more I thought about it, the more I was touched with pity for these people clinging with such desperate hands to a life that offered them nothing but work and fear, spawning their children into the manifold corruption of the streets.

*   *   *

Finally, we came to the Piazza Mercato and threaded our way through the vendors' stalls to the open door of the kitchen. As we stepped inside, I saw an old woman, filthy and in rags, sitting propped against the wall and holding out her hands for alms. One of her eyes was completely covered by cataracts, and both legs were amputated below the knee. Beside her was a little pile of five and ten lire pieces, the alms of the poor.

Peppino dug into his pockets for loose change and I did

the same. The old one made no gesture of thanks, only continued her monotonous whining plea. A group of boys from five to ten were playing ball between the barrows. One of them stumbled over her legs and she cursed him in mumbling dialect.

Inside the kitchen the light was brighter and the air was warmed by the glowing oven where the *pizza* was browning and the red sauce bubbled and heaved on the big pastry platters. The cook propped himself against the wall and mopped his face with a grimy apron. The tired-looking waiter leaned on the cash desk and talked to the *padrona*, a mountainous matriarch bursting out of her black dress.

There were half a dozen others sitting at the greasy tables, shovelling *pasta*, gurgling broth or sipping the raw purple wine that was tapped from the casks next door.

All of them were watching us with that sidelong speculative look which is peculiarly Neapolitan. Once again, I had been marked as a foreigner. I kept my eyes on my plate and made low-voiced conversation with Peppino.

One of the diners interested me. He was about thirty-five, with fine, well-chiselled, Roman features. His hair and his hands were well-kept. His clothes were new and his shoes were brightly polished. Yet he was eating here in a grimy kitchen patronised by barrow men and street girls.

I pointed him out to Peppino. He grinned at me, his mouth full of pizza.

"There are many like him in Naples today, Mauro. He is a little functionary—a clerk, perhaps, in a hotel or in a tourist office, or a salesman for one of the big industries in the North. He earns, if he is lucky, forty thousand lire a month, yet he must dress as if he were earning a hundred and forty thousand. That suit is possibly the only one he has and every Sunday he will sponge it and press it as if it were the most important thing in the world—which it is, for him. But to stay alive, to have enough money for fares and to buy a cup of coffee for his clients, he must eat here with the poor."

I had some idea of the cost of clothing in Italy, since shipboard accidents had ruined a pair of slacks and a hacking jacket. More from curiosity than from any desire to possess a skin-tight coat and a pair of cuffless trousers, I went to an emporium to enquire.

A cheap jacket, off the peg, would have cost me 13,000 lire; a pair of slacks, 7000; a pair of shoes of modest quality, 6000. Add the rest of the items—socks, shirt, underwear, a pocket handkerchief, a tie—and you have more than a month's income. A shoddy overcoat and another change of linen will eat up another month's income for my little functionary, and he still has only one suit to see him through three hundred odd working days.

"It can't be done," you say. It's true that it can't be done. But it is done, by hundreds of thousands of white-collar workers in Italy, today. It is done by means of a beneficent institution called the *cambiale*. The cambiale is, in fact, a promissory note. Every time I went to a small branch of the Banco di Napoli to cash a traveller's cheque or draw on my letter of credit, I saw dozens of people, men and women, signing or redeeming these insidious little documents.

The little functionary needs a new suit. He signs a promissory note which falls due in two months. The penalty for default being sequestration of property and a visit to the *questura*, he scrimps and saves and lives in daily torment to be able to meet the payment on the due date. If there is sickness in the house, or if a child needs school clothes or new text books, he signs more and more cambiali. Between the interest and the aggregation of responsibilities, he piles up debts that he can never hope to repay.

31

His rise in the world brings him no betterment. He is, in fact, worse off than the workers in the bassi, who at least manage to eat and who have nothing to lose from the whim of a senior official or the malice of an office rival.

Peppino's voice cut across the line of my thoughts.

"You're not eating, Mauro."

His own plate was empty and he was lingering on the last of his wine. My own meal was scarcely touched. The pasta was cold and doughy and the sight of it revolted me. I shrugged and pushed the plate away and drank my wine at a gulp.

"I'm not hungry, Peppino. I've had enough for one night. Let's go."

We stood up, walked to the cash desk, and, while Peppino paid the bill, I stood in the doorway and looked out into the crowded alley. The vendors were still crying their wares, although it was eleven o'clock. The beggar woman was still whining for alms and the boys were still kicking the ball around the barrows.

Suddenly, as if at a signal, they stopped and moved quickly down to the end of the alley. Only one remained. I watched him work his way back till he was level with the beggar woman. Then, with a single movement, he bent to the ground, scooped up the pitiful pile of alms and went racing away like the wind, between the barrows and into the warren of lanes at the end of the street.

The old woman wailed and the vendors screamed, while I stood there in the doorway, sick with indignation and disgust. The bassi of Naples are a jungle where only the strong or the cunning or the fleet of foot can survive.

Peppino laid a hand on my arm and drew me away.

"Scugnizzi, Mauro. The urchins of Naples. They, too, have to live. Let's go!"

I fumbled in my pocket and found a 1000-lire note which

I thrust into the hand of the weeping crone. She snatched it away and hid it inside the rags that covered her breast. Peppino and I walked away through the mud and slush and the rotting stalks of vegetables.

The voice of the beggar woman followed us like a malediction.

CHAPTER TWO

EVERY MORNING, during my stay in Naples, I would walk to a tiny park at the top of the Via S Teresa. Here, sitting on a stone bench in the sun, I would sort out my notes and the facts and figures I had collected the previous day.

Facts there were a-plenty. The figures were a different problem. Official Italian statistics are frequently false and always unreliable. This is a country which depends for its survival on the continuance of aid from America. The Government in Rome must make a regular reckoning with the State Department and the accounts are always cooked.

Here, in the South, there are twenty additional reasons for the cookery. Some of them I hope to make plain in this chapter.

Employment figures, for instance.

Official statistics declare 151,000 unemployed in Naples alone. It is my view, after weeks of investigation, that the figure is well on the wrong side of 200,000. The reason? The official figures take no cognisance of casual workers, seasonal workers or youths under eighteen, most of whom have left school before the age of twelve and all of whom

C.O.T.S.

B

must contribute in some form or other to the family maintenance. More than this, if a man carries a work card entitling him to function as a barber or a street photographer or a carpenter's labourer, he is, ipso facto, deemed to be employed. He has a profession. Why doesn't he practise it? He can obtain unemployment benefit only after stringent proof of starvation conditions, and he certainly can't be numbered among the unemployed.

When a boy leaves school—if he goes to school—he begins work at ten or eleven years of age. He is paid from 300 to 400 lire per day as an unskilled junior and, before he reaches eighteen, he is dismissed and thrown back on the labour market, half-trained and with no possible hope for the future.

Figures on education, too, make interesting reading. Italian law prescribes school attendance to the age of sixteen. Yet, there are 50,000 children in Naples who have no chance of getting any education at all, because there are not enough schools and not enough teachers.

Fifty thousand illiterates a year in a European city of two million is a horrifying picture. But the real facts are worse still. There are so few schools in Naples that even those who attend the primary grades can only be accommodated for two or three hours a day. In some areas they attend three hours a day *every alternate day*.

School attendance is, therefore, impossible to enforce, and in every street and lane of Naples you see children of school age running wild, ragged, dirty, uncared for, or pressed into service in shops or workrooms to augment the family income by a pittance every day.

There are other statistics, too, fearful enough for what they tell, but utterly horrifying in what they conceal.

There are, say the official figures, 7000 Neapolitan families living in hovels (*baracche* or *tuguri*). These hovels are

34

built on the sites of bombed buildings or in the shells of wrecked apartments, or even in grottoes in the rocks. Average the hovel families on the conservative Neapolitan scale of eight apiece, and you get 56,000 people living in conditions identical with the worst Eastern cities.

I was there. I saw them. For three nights I did nothing but walk round the baracche with Peppino. I saw fifteen people in one shanty sleeping under rags on an earthen floor. The men could not get work so they spent their days picking up tobacco butts for sale to the backyard factories at 1000 lire a kilo. Try working out how many trodden butts it takes to make a kilo of tobacco. The figure will surprise you!

At night the women went out and sold themselves on the streets while the children scavenged in the Piazza Mercato for food. Fixty-six thousand people live like that, according to the statistics.

But those who live ten in a room in the lanes of the bassi are not listed. They have homes with light and sometimes water. They are not qualified to join the ranks of the hovel-dwellers.

Figures! Figures! Figures! How do you make figures out of the monotonous litany of the miseries of Naples? I sat on my little stone bench and smoked a contraband cigarette and read the report of Budget Minister Adone Zoli from Rome. The date of the report was March 23rd, 1956. Minister Zoli was encouraged. Minister Zoli saw significant advances in the Italian economy.

Gross national income had risen 7·2 per cent. But in Naples 31,000 workers had been dismissed during the winter.

Private enterprise boosted its income 8·5 per cent. But in Naples an unskilled worker was lucky to earn 500 lire a day.

Agricultural production was 22·4 per cent above pre-war levels, and the cost of living had risen only 3 per cent. But olive oil, part of the staple diet of these people, cost 900 lire per litre, a rise of 50 per cent, and vegetables and fruit were nearly double last year's prices.

Figures! Figures! Figures! There were lies, damned lies and statistics, and they all told me less about the condition of this city than I could see with my own eyes.

I stuffed the notes into my jacket pocket, left Minister Zoli on the stone bench and set off on my daily tour of the city.

* * *

This morning I had an appointment—to drink coffee in the Galleria with a man who had a story for me. I had checked on him through friends. He was honest and respected. He is even well-known to many visitors who come to Naples and the bright islands and the tourist spots round the Sorrentine peninsula. To tell more than this would be an indiscretion and a breach of faith.

As we sat at a little cane table among the jostling, gossiping promoters in the Galleria, he gave me the story. It concerned the operations of an Italian Government Agency, through which American funds and Government grants are channelled to bolster the economy of the impoverished South. Its aim is to provide risk capital for Italian investors who are prepared to locate their projects here and provide work for the depressed thousands of the Mezzogiorno. So far, so good.

My informant was an investor. He owned and operated a first-class *pensione* in a tourist spot. He wanted to build a restaurant which would employ more of the locals and trap more of the tourist funds into the area. Again, a reasonable proposition. The building would give employment to local artisans, the restaurant would employ more staff.

More tourists meant more trade for the local shopkeepers and farmers.

Before lodging a formal application for the loan, he went to Rome and discussed the project with officials of the Agency. Their reaction was encouraging. He should file an application. He could rest assured of a favourable reply.

Ebbene! He filed the application. In due course there arrived a financial expert and a constructional engineer. They went over his plans with meticulous care. Good. They would present a favourable report. The rest was a matter of routine.

One month later, Mr X arrived.

Mr X was large, smooth and genial. He had a Roman accent and drove an Isotta of the latest model. He had come south for the sun. He would like a room looking over the bay. He got it. He stayed three days and, on the third day, he begged the favour of an interview with my investor friend.

They sat together in the private office of the pensione and Mr X laid his cards on the table. He was, he said, associated with the Agency. Not, you will understand, officially, but in the sense of counsellor, financial adviser.

My friend nodded cheerfully. His dealings with the Agency had been, to this point, more than cordial.

Mr X nodded too. The Agency was anxious to do all it could for investors in these areas. That was its function. However—

—However?

—However, said Mr X, there were many calls on the funds. There were many conflicting interests. In order to expedite the application and have the funds available in time to have the building ready for the next season, there would be necessary a small . . .

At this point, Mr X touched thumb and finger-tip together in the age-old gesture of the touting Neapolitan.

"How much?" asked my friend, tightly.

"Ten per cent of the amount of the loan, payable in advance in currency."

My friend was staggered. He was a Neapolitan, an hotelier to boot. He understood the refinements of squeeze and graft. But even he gagged on this one. He pointed out that at this rate the money would cost him seventeen per cent—a usual bank rate. The only point in getting a loan from the Agency was the low interest rate on risk capital.

Mr X shrugged. If my friend didn't get the money, he couldn't build his restaurant. Naturally he must make up his own mind. My friend made another obvious objection. He might pay the ten per cent and never see the loan. Mr X shrugged again. The risk was there, truly, but in these matters there was need of *fiducia*—mutual trust. Impossible to do business without *fiducia, non è vero?*

Our investor nodded unhappily. It seemed to him that it was impossible to do business anyway. He decided to play for time. Mr X was quite happy about that. The weather was fine. He would stay another day, even two. He would divert himself by a visit to Capri. Which he did.

While he was away, my friend sought counsel of his friends—bankers, lawyers, functionaries of the district. All of them advised him not to pay the money. Not, you will note, on moral grounds, but because of the danger of losing it. When I asked why he had not, for instance, agreed to make the payment and then have Mr X arrested by police witnesses, he shrugged. I didn't understand the way things were done in Italy. The chances were Mr X was a genuine contact man and that if he were arrested, it might be suddenly impossible to get cement and stone and building fitments. *Capisce?*

I understood. It was only another aspect of the corruption of commercial and political life in Italy today. Besides, I wanted to hear the rest of the story. It was interesting.

When my friend refused the payment, Mr X smiled complacently, paid his bill and left. After he had gone, our investor got busy again making the rounds of the money market. He could raise the money, surely, but under the prevailing system of discounts it would cost him up to seventeen per cent even from the Banco di Napoli. He was stymied.

Three months later, Mr X was back again, with the same big car and the same big smile.

His opening question had a Neapolitan flavour, in spite of the Roman accent.

"Are you cooked yet?"

"Yes."

"Then, why not pay like a sensible fellow and be done with it? I assure you, you'll get your money within a month."

"No!"

Even a provincial restaurateur can have his fill of gerrymandering.

Mr X smiled and took his leave. My friend wrote again on the matter of the loan.

He never got it.

When he built his restaurant, it was with private funds from an elderly friend at Salerno. The Agency was, no doubt, devoting the money to worthier causes—like the 7000 families rotting in the baracche, or the 50,000 children who cannot go to school.

I want to be fair on this point. Go to any country in the world and you pick up stories like this one. You check your informant and his veracity. Try to follow them through the departments concerned and you find yourself bogged down in a morass of conflicting statements and equivocal documentation. In Italy, however, they spawn like bar-room jokes. They are a symptom of the social climate. They reflect a profound mistrust of public administration. They breed cynicism and open the way for corrupt practice in high and low places. The paid lobbyist and the ten-per-cent contact man become stock characters in the political comedy and their smut brushes off onto the hands of honest administrators.

In case this sounds like a biased observation, here is a postscript from an ex-minister of Italy on the operations of a Government body whose official title is the Cassa per il Mezzogiorno—literally the fund for the South. He delivered it at a congress of the Rotary Club in Rome on April 8th, 1956.

'After a minute study of what happens to these hundreds of millions of funds, there is only one possible conclusion: the Cassa del Mezzogiorno is really the Cassa del Settentrione.'

The flavour of the pun is lost in English, but the meaning is blunt enough. The Cassa was set up to finance the depressed South. Its funds are being diverted to finance the industrialists of the North.

How much of them? According to Minister Corbino—who ought to know—nearly 70 per cent.

Sitting there in the dusty bustle of the Galleria Umberto, drinking my bitter coffee, watching the girls go by and the shabby little business men, looking at the shop windows filled with objects of art that nobody wanted to buy, I was oppressed by a despairing anger. I was angry at the injustice and the corruption. I was angry with my friend. I was angry with myself for becoming embroiled in the affairs of this ancient, worm-eaten, hopeless country, where men were bought and women were sold and the children were damned the moment they were begotten.

The children? They weren't my children. They weren't my country's children. They weren't America's children. They belonged to these same midday Italians who cheated and squeezed and oppressed one another and shut their hearts and their pockets against the cry that drifted up from the dark abysses of the bassi.

They are a Catholic people, as I am a Catholic, yet their social ethics areas pagan as those of Pompeii and the Rome of Tiberius. The slaves were manumitted centuries ago. But a man is still a slave if he is forced to live on the edge of starvation, to live in fear of the whim of an employer or an underling, with no possible hope of sharing in the fruits of his labour or improving the lot of his children.

Then a frightening truth began to dawn on me.

This poverty, this hopelessness, this corrupting fear, is in part a relic of history, in part an economic condition, and, in greater part, a thing calculated and organised.

The wealth of Italy—and there is wealth in Italy, make no mistake—is concentrated in too few hands: in the hands of the black aristocracy in Rome, in the hands of the great industrial families of the North, in the hands of people like the Lauro family in Naples.

The first aim of these people is to preserve their wealth, to augment it and then to divert as much of it as possible into safe investments abroad. The Kefauver inquiry revealed large Italian funds in American banks. My inquiries in Naples revealed at least one way in which these funds are sent out of the country in defiance of the law and every principle of social justice.

A permanent pool of unemployment is of advantage to such people. It keeps labour costs down and prevents agitation for better conditions. A permanently depressed area is a constant bargaining card with the Western powers, especially with America, whose fear of European Communism makes her specially vulnerable to these yearly assaults on her pocket. American funds poured yearly into Italy provide cheap working capital for Italian financiers; but, in the South at least, little of this money reaches the people whom it is intended to help—the poor, the workless, the children. There is a saying in the South that American money makes only a round trip—into Italy and out again, back to funkhole funds in American banks.

This fear of Communism is used in other fashions too. When a voice is raised against political corruption and social injustice, the speaker is branded a Communist and he is in instant danger of dismissal. The enunciation of the simplest democratic principles, which are accepted as a part of everyday life in Australia and America, raises howls of 'reaction' and 'Marxism' from a controlled and partisan Press.

Here in the South, it is not only the industrialists and the politicians, but the Church itself which is guilty. Ecclesiastical education is a century behind the times. Seminary teaching is unreal and reactionary and the constant proclamations of four popes have not yet penetrated into the dusty classrooms of the Mezzogiorno.

Men like Don Gnocchi and Padre Borrelli are phenomena almost miraculous and their lives are a daily battle for funds, for encouragement and systematic aid from the hierarchy and the civil authorities. It is to these men, and to others like them, that help should be given, because only through them will it reach the people for whom it is intended.

I said goodbye to my little restaurateur and left him, still wrestling with his own problems among the chafferers in the Galleria. The Via Roma was crowded and the traffic was a screaming horror. In this sprawling ant heap of a city I felt a little like Diogenes looking for an honest man. I felt sorry for the old philosopher. He had his work cut out.

Dozens of stories of graft and corruption came my way in the weeks of my investigation for this book. The stories themselves are less important than the climate which begets them. There is graft in every country. It breaks out sporadically like spring pimples; but the health of the body politic is not gravely damaged.

Here in Italy the case is different. The disease is widespread. The whole of society is sick with it. Everybody talks about it, but no one has yet found a specific to cure it. The social and commercial life of Italy is one gigantic skin game in which mutual trust and disinterested effort have become an impossibility for all but the heroes.

* * *

Among the good friends I made in Italy are two young journalists from Castellamare. Castellamare is an industrial town of some 60,000 inhabitants. It lies about half way between Naples and the tip of the Sorrentine peninsula, under the towering peak of Mount Faito. Eight thousand men are unemployed here because the shipyards are working at half speed and the canning factory provides only seasonal employment. Conditions in some quarters are as bad as any in the baracche of Naples. The boys had taken me round on tours of inspection. They had given me hours of their time, digging up facts, balancing my first impressions with explanations of the complex working of local government and local industry. Whenever I was in Sorrento, they would come to my house and talk till one in the morning. They were not only well-informed, but they gave me a useful check on my facts and conclusions.

One thing I noticed: it was impossible to discuss with

them or with any other Italian the simplest economic situation without constant reference to party factions and political cross-currents. It surprised them to hear that I had no intention of including in this book a discussion of multi-party politics in Italy. The only way to get anything at all done in Italy, they said, was to play the skin game, to use party influence. Even the best things had to be done that way. When I pointed out that the whole purpose of this book was to show what one man had done with faith, hope and charity and no politics, they shrugged and grinned uneasily. Like many young Italian intellectuals, they were violently anti-clerical and they could not see any good coming out of Nazareth.

I tried another tack. I told them how, in my home city, the young men of the Junior Chamber of Commerce—men of all religions and parties—had built, with their own money and their own weekend labour, a home for fifty old people and had pledged themselves to keep it in operation.

My friends agreed it was a good work, a work beyond the touch of politics. But here, in Italy, such a work would be impossible.

This I was not prepared to accept. What would be needed first? Land. Was it possible to buy a suitable piece of land in Castellamare? It was. The price? Two million lire. Would it not be possible to find two hundred citizens of Castellamare to donate 10,000 lire each (less than twenty dollars)? Possibly, yes. There was so much unemployment in Castellamare, would it not be possible to enlist voluntary help to dig foundations and cut stone and all the rest?

No. It would be quite impossible. The organisers would be branded revolutionaries and a dangerous influence. Their careers would be ruined and they themselves would be unemployed.

This was too much to swallow. Voluntary labour for

social betterment, self-help to provide a housing scheme for the old, the children. These were the most elementary steps in social reform.

"*D'accordo!*" My two friends couldn't agree more.

Instead of pouring out millions of words in 142 dailies about what the Government or the parties had failed to do, why not make a practical demonstration of what could be done with goodwill and courage?

Again we were wholeheartedly d'accordo.

Except for the fact that my two friends would most certainly lose their jobs, one as a correspondent and the other as a staff writer for a local journal. Quite possibly they would be arrested and charged as Danilo Dolci was charged with disturbance of the peace. And the house would never be built.

I was shaken, but I wasn't beaten yet. I pointed out that five years ago in Naples Padre Borrelli had started—from nothing—an institution for the reception of waifs and strays from the streets. I pointed out that the whole purpose of this book was to describe the circumstances which created the need and one man's heroic effort to meet it. If Borrelli had done it, why couldn't they?

They grinned. One of them pointed out that Borrelli was a priest which made it somewhat simpler. He couldn't lose his job. He might be disciplined but he would always eat. The other waved that argument aside. Mauro was right. Borrelli had started from nothing and had established this work. He had done much for the scugnizzi. He was an exceptional man and an exceptional priest. But even now, after five years, with Church approval and sporadic gifts from Government authorities, he was still selling scrap iron and old clothes to feed his boys!

There was no answer to that. I knew it. I had seen it with my own eyes.

Ten minutes later they went home and I went to bed. And a house for the poor at Castellamare seemed as remote and fantastic as Hy Brasil or the Golden Isles of the Hesperides.

* * *

I had another visitor, one sunny day, when I had come back to Sorrento to collate my mountains of notes and to wash the dirt of Naples out of my skin. His name was Don Arnaldo. He was a priest of the diocese of Naples. He, too, was a writer—a historian and a political philosopher. His latest work on the influence of Macchiavelli in Italian politics had caused quite a stir in learned circles in Europe.

Don Arnaldo had been a teacher as well—in one of the seminary schools which cater for a limited number of pupils in addition to the trainees for the priesthood. Several years in damp, unheated classrooms had left him crippled with asthma and periodic attacks of bronchitis. He was fifty-five years of age, he told me, but he looked older.

We sat in the sun on the terrace outside my study, looking eastward along the mountains, to the wooded shoulder of Capo di Sorrento. We drank German beer and smoked English cigarettes. We talked of the excavations at Castellamare and the Greek temples at Paestum and the early glories of the Republic of Amalfi.

Then we talked about the Church.

"We distinguish," said Don Arnaldo, in his careful, academic fashion. "We distinguish between the Church and its members: the Church, which is the mystical body of Christ, the repository of truth, the fountain of grace; and the members of the Church, priestly and lay, who use the truth and the grace well or ill."

I agreed to distinguish between the two. Philosophically the proposition was sound. Justice must not be confounded with the men who administer justice. Truth

46

is always truth in spite of the perversion of those who preach it.

The Catholic Church in Italy acknowledges the same head and the same body of doctrine as the Catholic Church in America, or Australia or Argentina. It gives the same latitude in cases of dubious definition both in belief and practice. That is the theory.

In practice . . .?

"In practice," said Don Arnaldo, unhappily, "I admit that the situation is different. A hundred years ago the Italian Church committed itself to an expedient—a cleavage, total and complete, from the political and social life of this country. She left the schools and the forum and the legislature. She accepted a dichotomy which is in fact a heresy—that religious life is one thing and social life another. There is only one life—human life in all its aspects. Man is a creature of divine origin and destiny. Every circumstance of his life, therefore, comes within the ambience of the Church. This is the doctrine which has been stated and restated by every Pontiff since Leo XIII, but the practice of it only now begins to be accepted by the body of the Church in Italy. Here in the South, acceptance has been the slowest of all."

"Why?"

"Because the Church of the South became linked with the rulers of Naples—Spaniards, Bourbons, the House of Savoy, one after another. The bishoprics of the Mezzogiorno became political perquisites. The prelates were, by breeding, conservatives, accepting the social order as a thing fixed and immutable. Now, we still carry on our backs the burdens of those troubled times. The new spirit is stirring, believe me, but it is like a plant in old, unfriendly soil, thrusting itself up through the rubble of history. It will take years yet before it grows freely in the sunlight."

I was angry and I attacked him. I had no right to do it, because he is a good man and a wise man and a gentle one, and he is many years older than I and knows a great deal more and is much closer to God.

I asked him what the people were to do while their tardy shepherds reformed themselves. I told him of the dusty friars and patient sisters who begged in the streets for funds to keep their orphans and their sick while wealthy Catholics closed their hearts and their pockets without a word of censure from any pulpit.

I asked him how Catholic employers could pay starvation wages to workmen and dismiss them at a moment's notice without protest from the prelates of the South. I asked him how the Church of Naples could tolerate the promiscuity of the bassi while refusing to preach the Ogino method of birth-control which is authorised by the Church. I pointed to the sallow-faced boys who were being trained for the priesthood in the seminary of Sorrento, drilled in the dated humanities of the nineteenth century, stuffed with the clichés of piety, segregated from the world, which one day they would have to teach and reform.

All this and more I thrust at him until my anger was spent and I began to feel ashamed of myself and was constrained to apologise. Then I poured him another drink and waited for his answers.

To my surprise he agreed with me.

"All that you have said, my friend, is true, though it does small justice to the active and enlightened men who are trying to change this state of affairs. It does less than justice to the many who, over the years, have built the orphanages and the homes and the refuges which are, even now, all that this poor city has of charity and relief. The Church in the South has committed many sins, but it has also done much good, and without it this people would be

48

sunk in a misery far deeper than that which they now suffer."

I nodded agreement. This too was evident. The Church, for all its shortcomings, is all that is left to the dispossessed of Naples. They look to it for help, for entertainment, for solace in the barrenness of their lives. It has given much. If it has not given more, it is because its members are human, burdened with human frailties, oppressed like the people of Naples with the sins of their historic fathers.

Don Arnaldo went on:

"The root of the matter is education. Education to produce an enlightened clergy who can speak with authority to the rich as well as to the poor. Education to produce educators, and apostles of reform and social justice."

I pointed out that the Church itself had control of clerical education. Bishops and archbishops directed their own seminaries and the training of their diocesan clergy.

"True," said Don Arnaldo, "but many bishops are old. Many more are conservative and afraid of sudden change. They admit the need of reform but fear the consequences of indiscretion in an explosive social situation."

"Then why not change the bishops?"

Don Arnaldo threw back his head and laughed.

"Come, come, my friend! You are not so naïve as all that! You know that there is a bureaucracy in the Church, older and more complex than the bureaucracy of this unhappy Italy. We have a Pope who is very near to being a saint—a great man and a wise one. Even he can only work with the instruments at his hand. To destroy an edifice is a simple matter. You can do it with a charge of dynamite. To replace it with a new building is the work of years."

I nodded and sipped my drink. To this, as to so many other problems, there was no easy answer. It was springtime in the South and the people were smiling because the

49

tourists were coming and the canning factories were working and there would be more work and more money, and the sun would warm their pinched bodies and the damp would dry off the walls of the bassi.

They are a patient folk. They have suffered much and they will suffer more. They have learned to be grateful for the smallest mercies. But I asked myself, as I had asked a hundred times before: the children—what of the children?

CHAPTER THREE

M Y ITALIAN friends used to smile whenever they heard me discussing this book.

"Naples is too big," they said, "too big, too old, too complex for you to understand."

I didn't agree with them. I still don't. Most of them had never been into the bassi. None of them had ever spent half as much time there as I had. Otherwise they would have known that life there is very simple, simple as birth and death and the act of love.

There are no mysteries in the bassi, only the mystery of how so many people stay alive on so little. Walk the streets by day and night and you will realise that it is physically possible to assist at every moment of the life cycle from conception to the dying breath.

Peppino and I did just that. It was my project to chart the life of a girl and a boy from infancy to maturity, to see what Naples made of them, and why and how.

Most of them, I am convinced, are begotten in love in the big brass *letto di matrimonio*, under the picture of the Madonna or the placid gaze of a plaster saint. The passion of the act tends to be inhibited by the proximity of so many people and displays of affection between married couples are rare. But there is much love in the bassi, and a strong respect for the marriage bond.

For the mother, the conception of a child is a joy. Later it will turn to grief, but in the months of her gestation, she is an object of interest and care and the centre of all the gossip of the street. Obstetric details are a constant delight to Neapolitan women and they are embellished with legendary details older than Pompeii.

The expectant mother will not normally go to a doctor. A single visit would cost her at least 1000 lire, and besides, gestation and birth are very normal functions, so why bother? It is a primitive state of mind which has some appalling results in later life, but many Neapolitan women seem to survive it without too much damage.

If there is an emergency which requires medical attention, no woman of the South would dream of going to a consultation without company. To undergo an intimate examination without an older woman present would be to compromise herself and the doctor. Even women of breeding and education follow the same practice.

Since no doctor will commit himself too far in front of a witness—especially a feminine witness—private practitioners are apt to deliver a Sybilline verdict, and the spread of gynaecological education becomes almost impossible. Rumour and gossip spread like forest fires in the crowded streets of the bassi and any doctor who set himself up as educator of his patients would find himself starving, or reduced to the shabby trades of the casino and the house of appointment.

Here, too, is the reason for the high percentage of messy abortions in Naples. An unmarried girl is apt to be complaisant with her fidanzato, because she is afraid of losing him. If she falls pregnant she faces family disgrace, possibly accompanied by a beating from her father or her brothers. If she is hunted from the house, she will end up on the streets. So, quite often, she addresses herself to the unscrupulous midwife, sometimes with horrifying results. By the time the doctor is called, it is too late for anything but drastic surgery.

When a child is born in wedlock, the mother is attended at home by the local midwife and half a dozen voluble, if unskilled, assistants. Her pain is public and her triumph is a matter of common rejoicing. Crowds of women gather outside the door and the men and the children are hustled away to a respectful distance, but the labour cries are strident and dramatic and even the children know what is going on.

Asepsis is primitive and always difficult. Mortality is high, but on this, as on so many matters of public welfare, accurate figures are hard to come by.

When the child is born and the mother washed and settled back in the big brass bed, the doors are opened and the procession of admirers begins. There is a strange and touching beauty about this primitive worship. The mother grey-faced and tired, with the child at her breast, the father twitching rough hands and grinning with nervous pride at the compliments of the neighbours, the children giggling and clambering on the bed to look at the new arrival, the midwife in the centre of gossiping women, the unmarried girls whispering in the corner all the esoteric details of the birth.

No matter that in a few years the child will be sprawling and scrabbling among the fishtails and the rotten fruit. No matter that the mother, worn out with parturition and poverty, will find herself barren of love for her large, unruly brood. In this moment she has the dignity of a queen and the homage of all the humble of the bassi.

Neapolitan children are breast-fed. Cows' milk is expensive and often of doubtful purity. The necessary additives are more expensive still. If the mother lacks milk, the child is fed by a wet-nurse, and since babies are born every hour in the bassi, these are not hard to find.

For the child this age of infancy is the best of his life. He is petted and coddled and the life of the household revolves around him. The unfortunate thing is that it doesn't last, and that the child can never remember it. Perhaps it is just as well. To remember the Lost Paradise in the slums of Naples would be an intolerable grief.

However, happiness, like misery, is a relative word and the infant in Naples has a rough time of it. He is warm and he is fed and he is loved. But his diet is unbalanced, and he is apt to fall an early victim to rickets or other deficiency diseases.

Late one afternoon Peppino and I stopped to talk to a youngish woman who was nursing a babe outside one of the half-doors in the Vico S Agnello. The child's face was covered with blotched and crusted sores of pellagra. I stopped to look at it.

"Ask her," I told Peppino, "does she know what that is?"

Peppino and the woman talked for a moment in dialect, then Peppino translated for me.

"*Malattia di pelle*—skin complaint. Lots of children have it."

I told him to explain to her that the condition was caused by dietary deficiency and could be cleared up quickly with vitamin complexes. Peppino shook his head.

"She would not understand, Mauro. You are wasting your time."

"Very well then, this is what we'll do. We'll go down to the *farmacia* and buy a bottle of vitamin tablets. We'll bring them back here and you'll explain to her what has to be done for the child."

Peppino grinned patiently, and again refused.

"You know what would happen, Mauro? She would take the bottle and hide it for fear of some evil influence. When her husband came home she would give it to him. He would take it to the black market and sell it for a sixth of its value. You would be wasting your money."

I was appalled at such ignorance. Peppino bent down and lifted a small ornament hung round the baby's neck. It was made of red coral and it looked for all the world like a miniature animal horn.

"You know what this is, Mauro?"

"Just an ornament. I've seen lots of them in the tourist shops and the jewellers."

"No, Mauro. It is not just an ornament. It is a charm against the evil eye. Who knows, one day this child may be out walking—it may even be sitting here as it is now, in its mother's arms—when along comes a man, like you, for instance, who has the evil eye—*Malocchio*. The baby could be struck blind, its stomach could turn sour, its hands or its legs might be twisted."

"Superstition! The same superstition that turns their honouring of the saints into a kind of idolatry."

Peppino smiled and spread his hands in deprecation.

"Sure, Mauro, sure! But superstition is a disease which you cannot cure with a bottle of vitamin pills. You need education for that."

Education! We were back to it again. Enlightenment, personal and social. But there were 50,000 children in Naples who would not be able to go to school, and hundreds more were born every day. Now it was my turn to shrug. I took out a packet of cigarettes and offered one to

Peppino, and we stood watching the young mother while she changed the child.

I needed the cigarette. The child had not been changed for a long time. The cotton napkin was filthy, and when it was removed the child screamed with pain. Its bottom was scalded and blistered raw. As a family man I have some experience in such matters. I was about to say something more, explain to the woman that——

"Come, Mauro!" Peppino took my sleeve and dragged me away. "If you are going to finish this work you cannot afford to break your heart in the first month. The child will live to scream again. And if not, you will not be able to change its fate even a little."

"But it's such an elementary thing—just common cleanliness. A child can't be left in its own filth any more than an adult."

"I know, Mauro. I know and so do you. But these people don't. And until there are people to teach them, they will never know. Would you like to come here and set up a school in the bassi?"

It was a fair question and I had to answer it honestly. No, I wouldn't like to come here. I knew it would break my heart in a twelve-month. I wouldn't have the courage. But unless someone had the courage, there would never be a hope for the mediaeval ignorance of the Mezzogiorno. In Naples it is bad, but when you go south into Puglia or into the mountains of Calabria, it becomes a destructive and an evil thing.

The land reform programme has been set back ten years by the primitive stupidity of the peasantry, and by the short-sightedness of the reformers.

When the first big estates were cut up and the share-croppers settled each on his own plot of ground, the local economy suffered a sudden collapse. Instead of the steward of the absentee landlord, who came eight or ten times a year to advise what to plant and where and what patch was to be fallowed and what cows were to be served, the peasant now had only himself to depend on. He had smaller grounds and he had to farm economically to earn a living. There was nobody to tell him how to spray the fruit trees or how to use the new modern fertilisers from America. He had land but no plough. He had to buy stock, and grain to feed them with. And in twelve months he had a new landlord—the local shopkeeper who rubbed his hands as he gave a little more credit and pocketed another document entailing the new properties.

The whole of the South needs education. It is a poor country, bone-poor. But if education and modern methods can open up marginal areas in America and India and Iraq, they can do the same here. The trouble is to find the educators. In a country where success at an examination depends in great part on the teacher's recommendation— often paid—there is little hope of building a trained nucleus of instructors. At present rates of pay the teacher is reduced to the status of a hedge-school dominie, and the heart is crushed out of him before he can get to grips with his work.

*　　*　　*

Now it was lunch-time and Peppino and I stood by one of the fruit barrows munching apples and studying the price cards. The question of diet was important in this study of the children and the best way to study the diet was from the price lists of the local dealers.

Eggs, which are sold everywhere, even in some tobacconists, were 480 lire a dozen. Even by Australian or British standards, this was expensive—nearly six shillings sterling. Bananas, imported from Somaliland, were 480 a kilo. New potatoes were 100 lire a kilo and spinach—poor and bitter because of the bad winter—was 100 a kilo. Apples, floury and bruised, cost 180 a kilo and even the local Sorrentine oranges cost 150.

Watching the local women, I found that they bought mountains of broccoli and spinach, a few onions, artichokes and, occasionally, carrots. Fruit they bought sparingly and in single pieces.

Across the lane, at the *salumeria*, butter was being sold for 600 lire a half kilo, and a loaf of bread for 60 lire. Put the daily wage for a worker's family at 500 lire and you'll see that there is little scope for balancing a diet and strengthening the children against deficiency diseases.

Meat of any kind is beyond the pocket of the worker—a half kilo costs more than a full day's wage. Pasta, the staple diet of these people, costs 300 lire a kilo. Salt is a Government monopoly and costs 120 lire a kilo. The cheapest drink is wine at 150 lire a litre—bring your own bottle!

Cooking presents another problem when you are providing for a community of ten in one room of the bassi. The poorest are reduced to cooking over a fire of charcoal or chips in a tiny dish, but most families have a tiny three-ring gas burner fed from a cylinder. The jets are small and the gas is of indifferent quality, so that any kind of varied cooking is an impossibility.

Small wonder that the harassed housewife falls back on pasta and tomato sauce and that children of six and seven could be mistaken for four in your country or mine.

I finished my apple and pitched the core on to a pile of papers in a dark archway. As I did so, I remembered that tonight, when darkness came, boys and girls would scrabble in that heap and probably eat the core that I had rejected. The thought turned me sick. Then my attention was diverted by another sight, common enough in the back streets. A tiny girl, five or six perhaps, was staggering along with a gunnysack over one shoulder. With her free hand she held a small, bare-bottomed toddler, with a filthy face and a running nose. Here, under our eyes, were the second and third ages of the children of the bassi.

The toddlers who have not yet learned to control their bodily functions trot about naked from the waist down, fair weather or foul. If it seems a barbarous custom to the mothers of our countries, let them ask themselves how they would cope with training a child—or even keeping him in clean diapers—in one room, without running water or a toilet. Of course the primitive hygiene also raises the death rate from pneumonia and tuberculosis—but what is one child more or less among the hundreds of thousands in Naples?

The little nursemaid herself was an interesting study. Her legs and arms were like matchsticks. Her hair was a tangled mop. She wore a torn dress of faded cotton under which hung a pair of pink knickers, filthy and ragged. Her feet were bare and her skin was blue with cold. I was clothed in long woollen combinations with an extra pullover under my seaman's jersey, but even I was cold in the thin spring sunlight that filtered down through the lines of washing! This tattered mite must have been frozen to the bone.

As she staggered along, bent under the heavy load, dragging the squalling toddler, she looked like a little old woman. I nudged Peppino. He called to her in Neapolitan, offering her an apple. She looked up immediately but her eyes were empty and there was no trace of a smile on her baby mouth. Peppino held out the apple in confirmation of his offer.

The child looked at him a moment in silent bitterness, then ducked her head and staggered away down the lane.

Now I began to understand what happened to the girls of the bassi. As more and more children began to be born, the older ones were pressed into service looking after the babes. While their sisters in other lands were playing with dolls or giving baby tea-parties on the lawn, these mites were washing the dishes and scrubbing the pans and sweeping the cluttered rooms with a twig broom. They were not sent to school, because there weren't enough schools, and besides, what use is education to a woman whose sole function is to sew and cook and bear children? They rose early and went to bed at fantastically late hours. I have been in the back streets at midnight and still found children playing on the cobbles. I have looked into the ground-floor rooms and seen them, at three in the morning, still fully clothed, sitting asleep over the kitchen table where their elders were talking.

Part of it is ignorance, part of it is thoughtless habit, part is the impossibility of maintaining an orderly life in the crowded rooms of the tenements.

The centre of the family is the father. He is the bread-winner. He comes home from work—if he has work—at nine in the evening. Then he must be fed and coddled a little, because generally he has done twelve hours labour on coffee and a crust of bread. By the time he is fed, it is ten, eleven, and the lights are still on and it is impossible to settle down in the big communal bed, until father and mother are ready. So the children sit late. If one or two or three are missing, they are presumed to be playing with the others in a nearby courtyard or under the lights near the vendors' stalls.

Their absence is a small mercy. After a while it becomes an unnoticed habit. By the time the corruption of the city has taken hold of the youngsters, it is a long, long way too late to mend it.

With the girls, the corruption works more slowly, if no less surely. Their childhood passes quickly, almost unnoticed. These years are spent in a round of domestic duties. They are close to their mother. They understand that this is a woman's life. If they laugh little and forget how to play like other girls, that, too, is normal and a thing not too much regretted.

It is when they reach the prickly, uncertain years of adolescence that the trouble begins. The warm propinquity of the marriage bed teaches them early the facts of life, while the tradition of honourable womanhood keeps them from any contact with young men of their own age, except the few who are admitted to the household as possible suitors and who must preserve always a rigid decorum.

Their young dreams begin to be centred on marriage with a good steady boy—a man who has work. It is one of the most pathetic things about this people. For them the good land is one where there is work and bread. They could not believe it when I told them I came from a place where there were more jobs than men.

Now the promiscuity of the family life begins to affect the maturing girl. Her first sexual contact is probably with an elder brother. It may not proceed to the act, though this is often the case. It is her only chance of sexual experiment without branding herself a dishonest woman.

Both the male and the female are inhibited by the abnormal conditions of their communal life and sometimes the secret contact becomes a habit. Even if it does not, however, there is left a deep sense of guilt, accentuated by their Catholic belief, and this guilt-sense has often worse consequences than sexual experiment outside the family. The spring is poisoned. The single secure unit begins to disintegrate and the girl or the youth is defenceless in the jungle of the bassi.

All this and more was explained to me by Peppino on one of our nightly jaunts. We had eaten pasta with one family and were on our way to the house of another where there was to be a reunion with music and possibly a little dancing. I led the talk round to girls and sex. Peppino put it bluntly:

"Consider, Mauro, what is the case with me. I have learnt from Padre Borrelli that there is no profit in a bad life or in a dirty one. But could I, at my age, live and sleep in a room with my sister when her breasts have grown and she begins to look like other women? If I am not to touch her, then I must find another woman to calm me. That means the back streets or the casino. Either way it is bad for me. The other way it is bad for her, also."

"But, Peppino, suppose—as it must often happen— your sister or a girl like your sister cannot find a good husband or an honourable marriage. Does she not have desires as you do?"

"*Sicuro!*" Peppino nodded, earnestly. "Our women are warm, too. If they cannot marry, then——" He shrugged. "It is the streets for them, or a man who will care for them even if he will not marry them, or the closed house or the house of appointment."

As we were talking, we were walking along a narrow dark lane which gave on to a small square in which was an old Spanish church. Just ahead of us one of the doors opened and a girl stepped out. As she stood a moment in the pool of light and turned back to say her farewells, I was surprised to see that she was well and fashionably dressed in a grey suit, with tan shoes and nylon stockings. She carried a modish handbag and wore a tweed coat of fashionable cut thrown over her shoulders. We slowed down to let her walk ahead of us, and I questioned Peppino:

"That one, for instance? She lives in this alley. Her

family"—I nodded at the doorway as we came abreast of it—"her family looks like any other. How does she dress so well and go out alone at this hour?"

Peppino made an expressive gesture.

"Perhaps she is like our little functionary. She has a job in a club or a restaurant or an hotel which requires her to be well-dressed. Perhaps all her family are in work— father, brothers—and they can afford to dress her. Perhaps she is not a good girl at all and has a room in the city where she takes men. Perhaps she is on call for a *casa d' appuntamento*. There are so many possible reasons. The only way to find out the true one is to ask the girl herself."

I didn't think there would be much profit in that. I told him so. I was more interested to find the answer to another question.

"Suppose, Peppino, that she is a girl who works the streets or the casa d'appuntamento. She still lives with her family. What then becomes of this honour of Naples, this care for the virtue of your womenfolk?"

Peppino looked at me sharply as if afraid that I was laughing at him. When he saw that I was deadly serious, he replied:

"There comes a moment, Mauro, in any family, when neither father nor brothers can control a woman. Perhaps there is so much need that they are grateful for what she brings and do not care to ask how she gets it. If it were your family, if you were workless and you lived, as the Neapolitans say, 'on the shoulders of your daughter', would you have the right or the courage to question what she did?"

I agreed that I probably wouldn't. I knew too many fathers who couldn't control their daughters even with a Jaguar and a private allowance. Who was I to judge the morals of Naples? I had the answer I wanted. I had followed the life cycle of a girl from the back streets. It led either to marriage or an unhappy substitute. Either way there was little hope in it.

In Italy today there are between two and three million women living by prostitution.

This is the figure given by Senator Lina Merlin, Italy's only woman legislator and sponsor of the new law, still battling its way through the Chamber, to close the brothels which operate under Government licence. The Senator claims that Naples is one of the three world centres for the white slave traffic and that operations here are directed by Lucky Luciano, gangster exportee from the United States.

It was my intention to include in this book a study of the operations of this traffic in Naples and the Mezzogiorno. The basic facts were easy to come by. The houses were open and were doing a roaring trade. Any hotel concierge or tourist tout would give you the address or telephone number of the houses on the Vomero where the call-girls operated. You would be shown a set of photographs and the girl who pleased you would be at your disposal in half an hour. From the scugnizzi I learned how they themselves touted for the girls and for the houses and were frequently recompensed in kind. In a city where girls can't marry because young men can't get jobs, the work of the recruiters is ridiculously easy.

But when I came to dig deeper, I found that I was being headed off at every corner. As an independent investigator, I found myself blocked by police and public officials. Italian journalists told me that they themselves were debarred from any enquiries into the trade. There were too many interests involved, too many houses being operated under dummy names by very respectable citizens.

Finally, a discreet friend in the police department pointed out that as a private individual, without the protection of an international news organisation, I might well end up in a dark alley with my throat cut. This I could readily believe. My scugnizzi friends had given me the same warning in different terms. Senator Merlin herself claimed threats against her life by the drug-and-dame cartels.

Reluctantly, I gave up the idea. But I had learnt enough to be able to write with truth and conviction this grim postscript to the story of the little girls of Naples.

The Italian Government admits that there are two million workless in this country. Take Lina Merlin's lowest figure and say there are two million prostitutes, many of them in closed houses operated under licence from the same Government. The two facts are directly related.

Poor men cannot marry. Poor girls cannot eat.

The pale-eyed pimps pick their teeth at the casino doors and make profit from both of them.

CHAPTER FOUR

ONE NIGHT, Peppino suggested that we go to the cinema. There was a good film showing. It was called *Il Kentuckiano* and the star was a famous American called 'Boort Lahncaster'.

Let me admit quite frankly that I love horse-operas and I can eat through a bag of popcorn as happily as any kid, while the Indians howl and the stunt men tumble in the dust. But Boort Lahncaster with long hair and an Italian accent was too much even for my juvenile tastes. I begged Peppino to suggest another entertainment—a *rivista*, perhaps, or even a puppet show.

He shook his head. This film was something special.

The place was special too—the Sala Roma. It was one of the meeting-places of the street boys and the others who did business with them. I wanted to study them, didn't I? I wanted to see what Naples did to them and how they acted after they left home and joined the scugnizzi? *Ebbene!* I must go to the Sala Roma. Besides, one of the boys there was a friend of his. I could get his story from his own lips.

We went to the Sala Roma.

It was like most Neapolitan film houses, a seedy-looking place with a dim foyer and garish posters. Boort Lahncaster was there, too, complete with deerskins and property wig and frontier rifle and a wolfish grin. My heart sank. Peppino grinned at my discomfiture and went up to buy the tickets. I stood outside and watched the patrons filtering in and the small knots of youths and boys strung along the pavement.

Most of them were shabby, as I was, but some of them were well-dressed in the current Neapolitan style, with short, tight coats and stovepipe trousers and bright ties and soft-pointed shoes, meticulously polished.

They were smooth-shaven and their hair was shining with grease, and I caught the whiff of lavender water and the profuse perfumery beloved of Italian barbers. I leaned against the wall and lit a cigarette and watched them.

They spoke loudly and volubly in high piping voices. Their gestures were wide and studied. Sometimes they would pat the faces of the younger ones or put an affectionate arm round their shoulders and whisper confidentially close to their cheeks. When they walked it was with the willowy self-conscious grace of young girls.

Then I knew who they were. These were the *femmenelle* —the odd ones. You will find them in every big city of the world, and in every city there are places where they congregate. The Sala Roma was such a place. I understood why Peppino had brought me here. He wanted me to see the end product of poverty, the shabby demi-monde in which the commerce of the streets is carried on, into which drift, finally and inevitably, the children of the slums.

The commerce varies: smuggling, pilfering, selling old clothes and German sun-glasses, touting telephone numbers, carrying packages of drugs from one Italian city to another. But the atmosphere is always the same—prostitution, perversion, dignity destroyed, a monstrous masquerade of spoiled humanity.

Peppino came out of the foyer and stood beside me. He jerked a furtive thumb towards one of the groups.

"That's my friend. Wait here. I'll have to talk to him first. This is business hours. I don't want to spoil anything."

I grunted agreement and watched him move away. It seemed to me that a change had come over him, that he was like an actor stepping out from the wings into the spotlight. He looked like one of those he was going to meet. He had the same attitude of cocky assurance and conspiratorial secrecy that characterises the Neapolitan *guappo*.

When he reached the group, he was greeted coolly enough. Only one of them, a weedy youth in a bright sun-shirt, showed him any cordiality. Peppino drew him aside and began a low, voluble conversation punctuated by gestures.

Peppino jerked a thumb in my direction. I looked away and tried to appear unconcerned, but from the corner of my eye I saw the other lad studying me carefully. Then he nodded, as if agreeing to Peppino's proposition. Peppino put a hand on his arm to lead him over to me; but he wasn't ready to come. He looked down the street in the opposite direction. He laid one finger on his nose and looked cunning. He jerked his head towards the foyer and rubbed his fingers together in the gesture that said 'money'. Then Peppino nodded and walked back to me.

"What was all that about?" I asked.

Peppino explained quickly.

"My friend is quite willing to talk to you. But first he has to meet someone"—he spat contemptuously—"a *pederasta* like these others. They have business together. Something about cigarettes. He says we should go into the film and he will meet us here when it is over. Then he will tell you all you want to know. He has a good story. *D'accordo?*"

"*D'accordo.*"

I was stuck with Boort Lahncaster. Nothing to do but make the best of it. The film was dull and the Italian dialogue made it duller. The theatre was dusty and full of cigarette smoke. Beside me a fat fellow snored spasmodically and belched garlic. In front a youth with greasy hair fumbled a girl as wide as a house-front. Peppino sat entranced through the whole boring melodrama.

When we came out, the little groups had dispersed and a chill wind was blowing papers along the dusty sidewalk. The boy in the flowered shirt was waiting for us. Peppino introduced us. Mauro West from Australia and Enzo Malinconico from Naples. Enzo suggested that we go to a bar. I said I would prefer to go to his place. He darted a quick glance at me, and Peppino explained hastily that Enzo lived in the apartment of a friend. His friend would be fastidious about being disturbed so late.

I can take a hint as well as the next man. I suggested a wine shop. Enzo suggested a kitchen. He was hungry. He had been working late. Ebbene, we would go to a kitchen.

We settled ourselves in a private corner. I indicated that I was the host. Peppino and Enzo ordered pizza. I contented myself with a glass of wine. While we waited for the pizza, Enzo began to talk. While he talked I watched him.

He was a small, narrow-faced boy with dark skin like an Arab's. His hair was straight and black and brushed backwards, flat against his scalp. He wore a black silk scarf under the flowered shirt. His hands were small and delicate, but the nails were broken and dirty. On the left hand he wore a large gold ring with a square zircon. When he wasn't talking, he was polishing this ring on the front of his shirt. Peppino told me later he was sixteen years of age. His eyes were twenty years older.

Peppino asked him how the business of the evening had gone Enzo went off into peals of laughter which ended in a spate of dialect. Peppino explained that Enzo had brought off a marvellous *combinazione*.

The other party was a pederasta, in fact the friend with whom he lived. This pederasta was the contact man for a group of smugglers. Tonight he had brought a consignment of three cartons of American king-size cigarettes to be sold by Enzo in the alleys off the Mercato.

Dutifully Enzo had gone off with the three cartons. Arrived at the Piazza Mercato, he had unloaded the cartons to another friend for 5000 lire. It was below the market price, but Enzo didn't mind. Everyone had to make a small profit otherwise nobody would stay in business.

I asked, innocently, what his friend thought of the deal.

Enzo laughed again and Peppino explained that this was just where the 'combination' was made.

Enzo had returned to his pederasta friend and explained with trembling fear that he had been stopped by the police and that the cigarettes had been confiscated. The friend was angry but there was nothing to be done. It was one of the risks of the trade.

So far, so good. Enzo was 5000 lire in pocket. But he

was not yet content. He was a clever fellow. He knew that the pederasta was afraid of the police, for many reasons. So he embellished the story. The police had asked him where he got the cigarettes. He said he had bought them from a man in the street. The police were not satisfied. Who could blame them? They had taken Enzo's name and address. Tomorrow he must appear at the *questura* for interrogation.

The pederasta was terrified. He had to be sure that Enzo would not implicate him. Enzo didn't want to implicate him, but the police were apt to be rough with scugnizzi, and even rougher with smuggling contacts. Enzo could take a certain amount of mishandling, but—again the familiar gesture—he would require some compensation for the trouble. The pederasta came through with 20,000.

Net profit to date—25,000.

Enzo and Peppino laughed again. I laughed, too. I needed the story. I had to pay with my small quota of applause. But there was more to come. The pederasta was a passionate fellow. He needed comfort. When he was frightened, he needed it more. These types were like women, *Capisce?*

Capito! Naturally, Enzo was prepared to comfort his friend, but tonight he was tired. More than that, he was becoming fastidious. This association with an odd one was beginning to worry him. He did not feel happy any more. It took another 10,000 to re-establish his peace of mind.

Net profit on the evening, 35,000 lire. *Bella combinazione, non è vero?*

Beautiful indeed. A comedy. I laughed dutifully. All the time I wanted to cry or heave my heart out in a quiet corner. I am a normal fellow with normal lusts; but I felt sorry for the slim, girlish invert, preyed on by the cold-eyed, calculating urchins of Naples. The girls were better off. The urchins brought them profit and were paid a reasonable percentage. But the odd ones whom God had made a little more than women, a little less than men, must pay and pay until they, too, were forced to sell themselves like the girls in the closed houses.

There was another side to the argument, of course. Not all the urchins were as knowing as Enzo. Not all were as old in years or in experience. Upon these the pederasti preyed in their turn, stripping them of the last shreds of innocence, turning them to darker trades yet and blackmailing them with the fear of the police and the fear of ridicule among their companions. In this shadowy, sub-human world, who was I to sit in judgment and say this one deserved pity and that a rigorous damnation?

Besides, this was no time for judgment. Little by little, with careful flattery, Peppino was drawing from Enzo the story of his life. I listened, spellbound. The story of Enzo Malinconico was the story of a thousand other urchins. The tragedy of it was the tragedy of all the nameless, numberless waifs who are known as the scugnizzi—the spinning tops—the wild, tormented boy-children of Naples.

Enzo Malinconico was the second son of a baker who lived just north of the Via Teresa. His father was old and hard-working, his mother was young: a not uncommon combination in the Mezzogiorno, where often the old ones are the only suitors who can afford to get married. When Enzo was ten, his mother took a lover. Before he was eleven, his father found out, went crazy with jealousy and committed suicide by burning himself in his own oven. Of his father, Enzo spoke with indifference. Whenever he mentioned his mother, he spat and called her *puttana*, which in Italy is a very dirty word indeed.

Soon after the father's suicide, the mother and her lover were married. It wasn't a very happy household. The mother was a harpy who harried both the boys and her new husband, goading them because they didn't earn enough and mocking them because they were living 'on the shoulders of a woman'. She herself peddled contraband cigarettes and was therefore a woman of some means!

Finally, the second husband committed suicide and Enzo and his brother were left as the sole providers.

The brother began to sell contraband. When the police picked him up and confiscated his stock, he went to work in the market. There he established contact with a small gang who stole cases of fruit from the loading lines and sold it later around Baiae and the Porta di Capua. Finally, the police picked him up again and sent him to the grim house of correction on the little island of Procida.

Enzo was now alone with his mother. He had not yet reached his eleventh birthday.

His mother put him to work as an apprentice to a local woodworker. He swept the floor and mixed the glue and carted the timber from eight in the morning till eight at night. In the evenings, his mother would fill his pockets with contraband cigarettes and send him peddling, until well after midnight.

One day Enzo ran away from home and never came back.

Every story I ever heard about the scugnizzi of Naples—and I collected well over a hundred dossiers during my investigations—came quickly to this first climax: he ran away and never came back.

You should understand that it was not hunger that drove them out. It was not always cruelty, as in the case of Enzo Malinconico. Sometimes it was overcrowding and the impossibility of living in a room full of squalling babies and drooling elders and quarrelling parents. More often it wus

71

the intolerable burden of work and family responsibility laid on the shoulders of very young children.

Just as the girls were made housewives when they should have been playing with dolls, the boys were made bread-winners before they had known what it was to be children. "At ten," as Padre Borrelli once put it to me, "they are too much men to be boys and too much boys to be men." Their bodies are stunted by this explosive psychological development and their minds are scarred irreparably by the early impact of adult life.

When, finally, they leave home, it is because they have come to the conclusion: 'I am the breadwinner. This family lives on my shoulders. It gives me nothing and takes everything. I am a man. I am better off if I live as a man—alone—and enjoy the fruits of my own labour.'

Enzo Malinconico left home with a pocketful of cigarettes and a few hundred lire. It wasn't a fortune, but it was enough to fill his belly and buy the toleration of a small bunch of boys who were touting for a casino. That night he slept with them on a stack of timber down by the Via Maritima. The next day he quarrelled with the gang and had his cigarettes stolen. He was alone and penniless and he was still child enough to weep.

A prostitute named Filomena took pity on him and brought him to sleep in her room. Her name, in Neapoli-tan, was Zizzachiona (the big-breasted) and her trade was among the dock workers and the sailors from the foreign ships. Enzo Malinconico lived with her for two years. He beat up trade for her and she paid him the regular percentage and when the last of the customers had gone, he crawled into bed and slept with her. With her he ran the gamut of sexual experience and learnt once again the venality of women and the corruptibility of men. He also learnt that the shrewd fellow is one who profits from both.

When he left Zizzachiona, he was thirteen years of age.

In the last three years he had graduated from laundry stealing and pick-pocketing to the more open and profitable commerce of the Sala Roma. Through the pederasta he hoped to be introduced to a man who needed couriers to make regular trips to Rome and Milan and Florence. The work was simple and well paid. You were given a package and an address. You delivered the package and came back.

When I asked him what was in the packages, Enzo put his finger on his nose and looked cunning.

"*Chi sa?* In this business the man who says least is the man who makes most profit. *Non è vero?*"

I grinned and said, "*Sicuro!*" and let the subject drop. The vices of wealthy Romans were no concern of mine. I was more interested in Enzo Malinconico and where he thought he was going. I asked him:

"Now, clearly, you are doing well. You have a head for business. But later? Where do you end? On Procida like your brother?"

Enzo's eyes darkened. His fists knotted. For all his huckster's confidence, in the bottom of his withered little heart he was afraid. Who could blame him? He was only sixteen. He said to me:

"My brother was unlucky. He was betrayed by a fool. Me, I am not going to end like that."

"How then?"

"In one year, two at most, I am going to have enough money to lease an apartment on the Vomero. One of the big new ones, with four bedrooms and a telephone. Then, I shall get some girls—not the *putane* of the streets, you understand, but girls of class and distinction, who dress well and talk well. We shall set ourselves up in business for the tourists, make contact with the best hotels, only the best. *Capisce?*"

"You mean a casa d'appuntamento?"

"*Senz'altro!* Certainly. In six months the *casini* will be closed under the new law which is going through the Chamber. Then will be the opportunity for the luxury trade."

"What about the police?"

"The police!" Enzo spat contemptuously on the floor. "How do you think the others function now? If you are prepared to pay, you can arrange anything in Naples. With four girls in a house of luxury, I can afford to pay even the police. Don't you believe that?"

I shrugged and spread my hands in the fashion of the South. It didn't matter a tinker's curse whether I believed it or not. If Enzo Malinconico didn't know his own market, who was I to tell him? If he made a mistake, there was always Procida, the grey stone island at the end of the long causeway. He would not be alone there. He would find his brother, and with him many another boy from the bassi of this doomed, dark city.

It was well after midnight when we left Enzo Malinconico and began working our way through the narrow lanes down towards the dock area to make the rounds of another collection of hovels.

We talked little. Peppino seemed strangely shocked by his meeting with Enzo Malinconico. It was as if he had heard once again the call of the streets and felt it whispering round his heartstrings, while all his reason and experience told him that to answer it would bring nothing but bitterness and disillusion. I was busy with my own problem: how to make people understand that what I would tell them about this city was the truth.

How could I convince them that the life of the bassi and the hovels was normal to hundreds of thousands of people? How could I prove to them that the story of Enzo Malin-

conico was repeated a thousand times over in this sprawling, maritime city where the Greeks had come and the
Romans and the Spaniards and the French, the Americans,
too, and the Spahis from Morocco, and where each had left
a part of his country's sins for the inheritance of the children? When I spoke of the casini and the houses of appointment, could they understand that I had seen twenty in
as many nights, with the lights burning outside and the
youths of the city rolling in for service?

This book would be read by gentlefolk in London and
in Ohio and in Melbourne, whose children slept soundly
between white sheets with teddy bear or a favourite doll
clutched in their arms. Would they believe me when I told
them that thousands of children played in the reeking lanes
till midnight and that hundreds slept in doorways or over
iron gratings?

How would they believe me in New York, when here,
in Naples itself, there were tourists and resident families
who smiled in polite disbelief when I told them what I had
seen? I didn't blame them. The tourists lived in the bright
modern hotels along the Via Caracciolo. The residents
lived in the villas of Posillipo or the post-war apartments
of the Vomero. They saw the Via Roma and San Carlo
and the broad square in front of the railway. When the sun
shone they went off to Capri and Ischia and the orange gardens of Sorrento. The tourists came for pleasure. The
residents wanted a comfortable life for themselves and for
their children. How could they sleep at night if they knew
the festering existence that began twenty yards from the
lights of the Via Roma and ended in the ugly ruins near
San Giovanni?

One answer was photographs. A single picture, say the
newsmen, tells more than a thousand words. I had com-
missioned a photographer to come with us and make

pictures of the things I had seen—the rags, the poverty, the squalor, the children who slept roofless and homeless in the bleak alleys of the bassi.

Suddenly Peppino stopped and tugged at my sleeve. He pointed to a narrow archway, inside which was an old stone well from which the dwellers in the rooms above drew their water in a wooden bucket at the end of a rusty chain.

In the narrow space between the well and the mouth of the arch, a child was sleeping. A boy-child, six or seven years old. His only clothing was a ragged jumper and a pair of patched trousers that reached only half way to his knees. He lay on his side, his bony knees drawn up under his chin in a foetal attitude.

We moved closer. Peppino struck a match. In the weak yellow light, I saw the matted hair and the dirty face and the blue blotches of cold on the wasted limbs. I felt hot tears scalding my eyelids. Peppino looked up at me. I nodded, but I could not speak. The match guttered out. Peppino handed me the box and motioned me to strike another. Then he knelt down and wakened the boy.

He sat up with a start, a pitiful wide-eyed creature, tense as a cornered animal. If Peppino had not held him, he would have bolted away into the shadows. I could see his bony chest heaving under the tattered clothes. I struck one match after another, while Peppino talked to him in soothing tones.

Where had he come from?

"Rome."

"Rome?" Even Peppino was startled. Rome was 150 miles away. But when he repeated the question, the boy nodded vigorously.

"Rome."

"How did you get here?"

He had walked, it seemed.

"All the way?"

Most of it. Sometimes he had ridden on a cart. Then he tried to get on a train, but the men chased him off. Then he had gone into the tunnels, and come into the city that way.

The *sotterraneo*! Peppino shook his head. The horror of it was too much even for him, and he knew, none better, the harsh shifts of the urchin life. Again he talked to the boy, telling him that there was a place where he could sleep in a bed and eat good food and where people would be kind to him. Would he come? The boy refused. He began to struggle, wildly, like a trapped bird. Slowly, patiently, Peppino calmed him, coaxing him from panic to tears and from tears to doubtful wonder. Finally he agreed to come.

For once in Naples I was glad that I was a big man. I lifted the tiny body in my arms and carried him all the way back to the House of the Urchins.

And that was how I came to know Antonino, the child who has haunted my nightmares ever since.

PART TWO

LIGHT IN THE DARKNESS

CHAPTER FIVE

Now I want to show you a man.

He is small like all Neapolitans. His height is a meagre five feet six inches; his body is tight, stringy and compact. His feet are small, his hands too; but these are horny and rough like a workman's. He has jug ears and a mop of curly hair, unusually fair for a man of the South.

His face is lean, with a wide, thin mouth that opens betimes in an urchin grin, or shuts like a tight trap when he is angry. His beaked nose is broken and pushed to one side of his face, and this, with his bright, intelligent eyes, gives him a strangely birdlike look.

His voice is well-pitched and vibrant with conviction. When he talks of Naples and the children of Naples, his speech is full of a terse and vigorous poetry. When he lapses into dialect, his accent is that of the bassi from which he sprang and whose horrors he has endured in his own thin body.

He is thirty-five years old and his name is Mario Borrelli. Of all the men I have ever met, this one is most a man.

He is also a priest; but the long soutane and big platter-like hat match oddly with his crooked larrikin face. Yet, he is a good priest, as he is a good man. When you come to know him better, you may even judge that he is a great one.

Mario Borrelli was the son of a labourer in the slums of Naples. He was one of ten children who lived, as I had seen the others living, in the crowded, insanitary conditions of the back-street tenements.

When the war began he was a clerical student, in no wise different, so far as I have been able to find, from any one of the pale pinched youths one sees today in the old-fashioned seminaries of the City of Naples.

When the war ended, he was a priest, one of the hundreds one sees every day walking the streets in dusty black, preaching his Sunday sermons to the pitiful congregations of the poor, sitting in the dark, smelly confessional for the weekly litany of sins, shuffling the dying through their grateful exit from the world, baptising the children who were born so hopelessly into it.

This was the bad time in Naples, when the city lay prostrate in the inertia of defeat, when the girls of the city prostituted themselves for the bread of the conquerors and the men of the city ate it with bitterness in their mouths. This was the time when the word of God was hideous mockery —to the humble who had been twice betrayed, to the mighty who were preparing themselves for a new betrayal.

How could you preach the Sermon on the Mount to the starving and disillusioned poor? 'Blessed are the meek . . .' when only the strong and ruthless could survive? 'Blessed are the merciful . . .' when the conquerors ate chocolate while your children cried for bread? 'Blessed are the clean of heart . . .' when fathers peddled their daughters to the Allied troops? 'Blessed are they that hunger and thirst after justice . . .' when all you knew was belly-hunger and the cold of the ruins eating into your bones?

Small wonder that young priests despaired and old ones settled themselves back into the apathy of formalism, which is the despair of the aged.

By 1950, the city was beginning to recover. There was the beginning of order, the beginning of work. But the relics of war were everywhere. I was here, I saw them. What existed in 1956 was bad enough, God knows, but then it was much worse. The demoralisation of the children, the homelessness, the despair, was evident even to the tourist. Now he sees less of it, and need not see any if he stays on the Via Caracciolo or lets the tourist guides steer him away from the bassi.

In 1950 Mario Borrelli began his work. When I asked him why and how, he shrugged eloquently.

"I was angry. I was bitter. I knew that I could not remain a priest, unless I did something worthy of a priest. I could not stand at the altar and hold the body of God in my hands while the bodies of his children slept in the alleys and under the barrows in the Mercato."

"Why the children?" I asked him.

He stared at me in amazement.

"In God's name, who else? For the men and women it is bad enough, but for the children it is a nightmare! How are we to begin, if not with the little ones?"

"How did you begin?"

He gave me a sidelong, Neapolitan grin and shrugged expressively.

"That, my friend, is a long, long story."

Then he told me. But the story I give you here is not the narrative of Padre Borrelli. He is a discreet man and a loyal one. Also, I believe, he has to be careful. The helpers in Naples are few; he still depends on a minute trickle of charity and the sporadic support of wealthy people, with a small stipend from Rome. He cannot afford to be too outspoken. His boys need him still. He has made them a home and given them hope. But in 1956 they were only two steps away from the dark streets from which he snatched them.

* * *

One day, towards the beginning of 1950, Mario Borrelli presented himself for an interview with his ecclesiastical superior, Cardinal Ascalesi, Archbishop of Naples and Primate of the Mezzogiorno.

He was twenty-eight, then, remember, a youngster from the bassi with the oil of his anointing hardly dry on his nervous fingers. Ascalesi was an old man, wise in the world and in the Church, burdened with the manifold distresses of his people, with political intrigues, trying desperately to buttress the crumbling Church of the South with his own aged shoulders.

He listened, patiently, while Borrelli made his request.

It was an odd one in any language. He wanted to take off his soutane. He wanted to go out and live in the streets with the scugnizzi. He wanted to understand their lives, their psychology, to make himself their friend, one day, perhaps, to bring them to live with him and teach them to live decently.

The old Cardinal pursed his thin lips and frowned. Was there perhaps a taint of heresy in this young priest? If not of heresy then of pride which would destroy the work and the priest with it? The life of the streets was a foul and evil thing, founded on venality and sensual sin. How could a young man expose himself to it and remain unstained? He put these things to Borrelli.

The young man's answer was simple. He had thought about it a long time.

"Ever since I entered the seminary I have been taught that a priest must make himself *alter Christus*—another Christ. It is written in the gospels that Christ ate and drank with thieves and street women. How can a priest be wrong if he does the same? How can he be another Christ if he refuses to go down to those who have no shepherd?"

Ascalesi was moved. With more men like this one he

might have succeeded in reforming the Church of the South, but now it was late in the day and he was growing old. He shook his head.

"No, my son. No! Before we can begin new works like this one, we must set in order what we have already—the parishes, the schools, the orphanages. There is work under your hand. Do that and rest content that you are serving God as he wishes to be served."

Borrelli was angry. Because he was a Neapolitan, the anger was swift and incontinent.

"Your Excellency does not understand. How can he, when he does not see? These are children, the little ones of Christ! They sleep on the gratings and in the beds of prostitutes. They pimp and steal and lend themselves to murder and violence. They live like animals in the forest, friendless and alone. And Your Excellency tells me to forget them. For what? For those who have faith already? For those who have homes? For those who are cared for in the orphanages? No! If the Church refuses this work, it is not the Church of God!"

Old and grey and terrible, the Cardinal sat in his high-backed chair and looked down at the small, boyish fellow who challenged him; challenged, too, the ancient power of the Church which he represented.

What did he think? Did he think of Paul withstanding Peter because he held to the Jews when the Gentiles thirsted for the faith? Did he think of Vincent the Frenchman who sold himself to the galleys to join the forgotten and the desolate? Did he think of the gentle Francis whose frail shoulders held up the tottering Church in the old days? Did he think of the reforms he had not made because he lacked the strength and the men to help him?

He is dead now and he cannot tell us.

White-faced and trembling, Borrelli waited. For him,

too, this was a crisis. If to be a priest of Christ meant to desert the children of Christ, then, he felt, he did not want to be a priest. It seemed an age before the old man spoke again. His voice was strangely gentle.

"To redeem the children is one thing. To take them off the streets and give them a home—this I can approve. But the other—to live with them on the streets, to become in a sense a partner in their misdeeds—this I cannot understand. Why do you want to do it?"

Borrelli relaxed a little. There was still hope. He took a deep breath and plunged into his explanation.

"Your Excellency, you must understand something of what the life of the streets does to these children. You must know that to be a scugnizzo is to have a man's soul in the body of a child. It is to have suffered in that body the rape of innocence, the pain of hunger, the bleak, desert cold of the city. To be a scugnizzo is to live without love, to trust no one, because the one you trust will snatch the bread from your mouth or the cigarettes from your pocket. To be a scugnizzo is to know that every woman is a whore, and every man a thief, that every policeman is a sadist and every priest a liar. If I went among them as I am now, they would laugh at me or spit in my face. If I offered them a home they would tell me that the carabinieri offer them a home, too—in a house of correction. I should never come within a hand's reach of them. Believe me, Your Excellency . . ." His voice trembled and he threw out his arms in a passionate gesture of appeal. "Believe me! I was born in the bassi. I know!"

Cardinal Ascalesi sat in his high-backed chair and pondered. Once in a lifetime, if he is fortunate, twice, if he is singularly blessed, a bishop finds among his clergy a man so marked by God that to turn him away would be like turning away Christ himself. This Borrelli looked like such a one. What he asked was strange, but exceedingly simple, new but old as the Gospel. It was not to be denied lightly nor yet accepted with haste and indiscretion.

The old man laid his hands together, fingertip to fingertip and pursed his grey lips. Then, softly and deliberately, he gave his verdict.

"I need time to consider this matter. Come back to see me in ten days. Meantime——" His voice faltered a little and his tired eyes softened. "Meantime, pray for me, my son. Pray for both of us. You may go."

Mario Borrelli walked out into the dusty sunshine of the city, puzzled and unsatisfied. He was too young to know how deeply he had touched the heart of Ascalesi. He was too afraid to see how close he was to success. More than this, he was a Neapolitan and he knew how often a polite deferment meant a definite refusal.

He knew then, what I have since proved from my own brief experience, that, to one who has not seen it with his own eyes, the life of the bassi and the plight of the children is a bizarre nightmare, a dramatist's creation, not to be taken literally.

The Cardinal sat in his big palace attended by discreet and subtle advisers, the bureaucracy of the Church. How could he understand what went on in the back streets? The problem was to make him understand, so clearly that no adviser could talk him out of it.

Mario Borrelli went home and prayed. That night, as he lay wakeful in his narrow bed, the idea came to him. He looked at his watch. It was still an hour to midnight. Time enough yet to make contact with the man he needed. In a flurry of excitement, he slipped out of bed, dressed himself, left the house and hurried to the nearest bar to make a telephone call.

An hour later, he was drinking coffee and talking excitedly with a photographer from a Neapolitan daily. The project they framed was shatteringly simple.

In the ten days and nights that were left, Borrelli and the photographer would walk the city together. They would photograph what they saw—the homeless waifs sleeping in the streets, the urchin packs cooking the food over fires in the alleys, the nightly interrogations in the questura. Then they would show the photographs to Cardinal Ascalesi.

Ten days later, Mario Borrelli stood before the old man and watched him poring over the glossy prints spread out on the desk. The Cardinal's face was haggard as he scanned the devastating evidence before him. Then he straightened up and spread his hands over the photographs, as if to shut them out of his sight. His grey mouth was tight with anger. When he spoke his voice was strong with conviction.

"Even had you not shown me these, I should have given you permission for your work. Now that I have seen them, I am doubly sure that it is a good work. But . . ." Ascalesi paused and Borrelli waited tensely for the rider. "But I am still sure that this work is full of danger—spiritual danger—for the man who undertakes it."

Borrelli nodded. He knew it himself, very well. He was a Neapolitan, young and warm-blooded. How would his priestly vows stand the impact of the thrusting sensuality of the streets? It was a question he had asked himself many times.

Ascalesi went on:

"Therefore, I consider it wise that you should have a companion, not necessarily for this pilgrimage of the streets but for the project in general. He should be a friend as well as a counsellor, so I leave you free to choose him for yourself and recommend him to me. I shall relieve him of his present appointment and attach him to you." The old man's face relaxed into a warm smile. "David goes out to fight Goliath in the streets of Naples. As well that he should have a Jonathan to comfort him. *Non è vero?*"

Borrelli's tight face broke into an urchin grin. He felt free and happy, and, like all his people, he wanted to shout and sing and tell the whole wide world. But the Cardinal was a great man and demanded a great respect. So Borrelli mastered his joy and began to tell the Cardinal of his friend, Spada, young like himself, a priest of the diocese of Naples. He was not, like Borrelli, a thrusting, combative man, but his heart was full of love for children, and when the urchins came one day to the house they hoped to have, they would have much need of love and fatherly care.

The Cardinal nodded his approval of this line of reasoning and began to talk of other matters. One hour and a half later, Mario Borrelli stood in the streets of the city and looked about him. It was his city now and the children of the city were his children. If he failed them, there was no one else to whom they could turn. He shivered though the sun was warm. He felt suddenly lonely and afraid.

He turned into an old grey church and knelt a long time in prayer.

* * *

A few days later the scugnizzi of the Piazza Mercato turned a speculative eye on a new arrival.

He was working his way up from the direction of the waterfront, picking up cigarette butts as he came. He wore a filthy shirt, patched in many places. His trouserlegs were ragged and hung down over a pair of odd shoes, cracked and broken at the seams. His hands were stained with grease and tobacco. His face was grimy and unshaven and he wore a greasy peaked cap on the back of his head.

At the corner of the Piazza he stopped, leaned against the wall, took out a half smoked cigarette and lit it with a wax match that he scraped against the stone. He smoked slowly, shoulder against the angle, legs crossed, bright eyes darting this way and that appraising the trade in the Piazza.

The boys studied him carefully, noting the broken nose and the tight mouth and the insolent tilt of the head. A guappo this one—cocky, tough, dangerous possibly. They hadn't seen him before. They wondered where he came from, whether he were alone or whether he were a scout from one of the groups operating down by the merchant docks. Was he buying or selling? Was he a contact man beating up trade for someone else? In the world of the scugnizzo these were important questions closely related to the economics and politics of the half-world. It was important to get the answers as soon as possible.

They let him smoke for a few moments and they studied every gesture he made. They saw how he held his cigarette between the thumb and the forefinger. They saw how he blew the smoke out of the corner of his mouth. How he spat into the puddle, how he cleaned his nose by pinching it between two fingers and then wiping it on his sleeve. They saw how he scratched his thighs and his armpits like a man accustomed to lice in his clothes.

No doubt about it, he was one of the boys. Now it was time to make contact.

A weedy youth with a dark, Arab face detached himself from one of the groups of loungers and sauntered across the Piazza. Out of the corner of his eye, Borrelli watched him come. His stomach knotted a little, but no flicker of fear showed itself in his bright eyes. The youth came abreast, opened a packet of American cigarettes, stuck one in his mouth, shoved the packet into his pocket and then asked for a match. Borrelli took the glowing butt from his mouth and held it against the tip of the other's cigarette. Then he put it back in his own mouth. He did not move from his lounging posture.

The youth grunted his thanks and leaned on the wall beside Borrelli. He spoke out of the corner of his mouth in the slurred and sing-song dialect of Naples.

"I haven't seen you before."

Borrelli shrugged expressively.

"Naples is a big town. I haven't seen you either."

The dark youth blew out a cloud of smoke and considered the matter. The accent was right, the words were right. You can't fake the dialect of the streets. The attitude was right, too. The fellow was a guappo all right. You couldn't rattle him. Best to take him easy.

"You in business?"

"Sort of."

"Got any contacts?"

Borrelli cocked his head on one side and gestured vaguely.

"Enough for me."

"What sort of contacts?"

Without haste, Borrelli fished in his pockets and brought out, in succession, a packet of American cigarettes, a cheap ring with a synthetic stone, a dollar bill and a grimy address book with a few scrawled names and telephone numbers. The sallow youth studied them a moment, then nodded approvingly. Contraband, theft or receiving, a few girls. It was enough for one man. This one obviously knew how to look after himself. But there was something else he had to know.

"Ever been in gaol?"

Borrelli grinned, crookedly, and spat on the ground.

"Not yet. But I need a change of air."

Ah! Now we were come to the nub of it. The police had been on the tracks of this fellow, so he was moving his camp. That made him more co-operative, more susceptible to a proposition. The youth fished in his pocket and brought out his own cigarettes.

"Here, have one of these."

Carefully, Borrelli pinched out his own stub and put it in his pocket with the rest of his gleanings. Then he took a cigarette from the proffered packet.

"Thanks."

"What's your name?"

"Mario."

"Mine's Carlucciello. I run things round here." He waved an expansive hand at the seedy bustle of the Piazza Mercato. "Like to meet some of the boys?"

"Sure."

Mario Borrelli heaved himself off the wall, hitched up his belt and sauntered across the crowded square with Carlucciello. His face was still the cocky indifferent mask which the guappo presents to his fellows. But inside he was grinning like a schoolboy. He had passed the first test. He was in.

Mario Borrelli had become a scugnizzo.

* * *

Now there began for him a life that was a grotesque parody of normal human existence. He had entered the kingdom of the beggars. He had taken on their dress, their speech, their habits. He must turn now to their shifts and stratagems to keep himself alive.

The gang in the Piazza Mercato had accepted him. He must make his just contribution to their harsh life. He must accept their risks and their devious code of honour.

So the moralist became an associate of thieves.

When the more agile were scaling balconies to steal washing or tools or the pitiful jewellery of the poor, Borrelli kept watch and whistled the warning signals. When the proceeds were sold to the fences, Borrelli added his voice to the chaffering and held out for a better price.

When the boys were chased by angry householders or the police, Borrelli carried his share of the spoils and ran like a hunted animal. He ate the bread that was bought with money stolen from Church poor boxes. He peddled the cigarettes that were smuggled through the customs or filched from the glove-boxes of American cars.

The celibate joined the pimps.

He was one of the dancing groups that edged the foreign soldiers closer and closer to the casino. When the girls came out to sun themselves on the balconies or at the doors of their shabby rooms, he talked with them and joked with them. He took his share of the money that was paid in commission by the whoremasters and by the private practitioners.

The priest became a beggar.

He stood with the boys outside the tourist agencies whining for cigarettes. He carried bags and jostled for tips. He collected trodden butts and teased out the tobacco for the back-alley manufacturers. He opened car doors outside the theatre and was jostled and pushed by the fine gentry who were affronted by his filth.

When midnight came and the commerce of the day and the night was done, he squatted with the scugnizzi over a fire of twigs and warmed his scraps of food and talked with them in the argot of the streets. He slept huddled against them for warmth, under the stairways or in the corners of the courtyard where the wind was less.

For four months he lived this life, and the marks of it are on him still.

When I pressed him for details of his urchin life, he shrugged uneasily and refused to give them. It was 'fastidious' to him, he said, using the Italian phrase. It embarrassed him. He preferred to look forward, not back. What I learned about him was told to me by the boys who had shared his life and the love he poured out on them even in the tormented existence of the streets.

He is quick to anger when anyone makes a slighting remark about the poor, or the shabby trades of Naples. He speaks with a Christ-like gentleness about the girls in the closed houses and in the poor back rooms. His fiery indignation pours out on those who profit from this commerce in flesh and misery.

But it was not until I probed deeper and more brutally that I touched the real wound. It is not healed yet. I do not think it will ever heal.

As a Catholic priest, Borrelli believes and preaches that the end can never justify the means, that it is never lawful to do a wrong act even to compass a worthy one.

One day, I put it to him bluntly:

"You are a priest, Don Borrelli. How did you square your conscience with your actions as a scugnizzo?"

He looked at me sharply. He had been interviewed by many people, but I was the first, I think, who had probed so close to the core of the matter. It was a long time before he replied. When his answer came, it was pieced out with meticulous care, as if he were trying to explain it, not only to me, but to himself.

"It was my endeavour, so far as possible, to withdraw myself from the direct act of sin. For instance I never stole, personally. I never solicited directly for a girl. I participated, certainly, in the act, but I tried so far as possible to make my participation a matter of appearance, to withdraw it, as much as I could, from the substance of the act."

"But in fact you did participate?"

"Yes."

"And you did share in the fruits of the act?"

"Yes."

"Was that justifiable in law and conscience?"

Borrelli pushed a tired hand through his hair and looked at me steadily. I was ashamed of my insistence but, if I were to arrive at the truth of the man, I must have the answer. He gave it to me, quietly.

"Much of it was justifiable, yes. Much of it was, shall we say, on the razor edge between right and wrong. But I was committed, you see, I could not turn back. I could only make my own judgment and commit it to the mercy of God. Even so . . ."

He broke off and looked down at the palms of his workman's hands.

"Even so?"

"Even so " said Don Borrelli, softly, "there were many moments when I was a scugnizzo and not a priest."

I did not ask, because I had no right to know, what were the things for which he reproached himself. But my heart went out to him. No matter what he did, no matter how much good flowered under his hands, he would always be haunted by those moments when he was a man and not a priest. Perhaps it is the Almighty's way of saving the best of his servants from the ruinous sin of pride. I don't know.

But I do know that God will judge Mario Borrelli a lot less harshly than he judges himself.

CHAPTER SIX

MARIO BORRELLI had two things in his mind when he went down into the dark kingdom of the urchins: understanding and leadership.

Without understanding, he could not lead. Unless he led, he could not hope to survive the climactic moment

when he revealed himself as a priest and offered the scugnizzi a home and a hope.

So, during the nights and days of his masquerade, he set
himself to study the nature and character of the street boys
—their needs, their hopes, their fears, and their reactions to
normal existence. His findings were passed on to me in
hours of earnest explanation.

Most of the time I had with him was at day's end, before
I went on my nightly rounds with Peppino. Often it
wrenched my heart to see him haggard and tired after a
day's hawking and begging, badgered and bedevilled by
accounts that wouldn't balance and bills he couldn't pay.
Yet, when he spoke of the scugnizzi, his eyes would light
up and his voice, too, and he would stride about the room,
gesturing in impassioned exposition.

"To understand these children, my friend, you must
understand first what it means to be a Neapolitan. We are
not Italians. We are a different people. We are a mixture
of many, and yet we are one. Look at our faces! This one
is swarthy and narrow like an Arab. That one is pure
Roman. This girl looks as though she has stepped from a
Greek vase of the time of Pericles. We have the red hair of
the Lombards and the blonde hair of the Germans." He
grinned, boyishly. "Some of us now have the black skin of
the American Negro. Yet we are all Neapolitans. We are
boastful like the Spaniards, subtle like the Etruscans, greedy
like the Bourbons. Like the Arabs, we have need of God.
Too often we say our *Aves* like the Arabs say '*Inshallah!*',
then squat on our haunches and wait for a miracle. Listen
to our songs! They will tell you what we are. We are arro-
gant, we are humble. We are grasping, we are generous.
We are simple, yet devious. We are languid and we are
passionate. We are changeable as the sea, yet we have endured like the sea and like the sea we are always the same.

But . . .!" He stopped his pacing and swung round to me with a dramatic gesture. "There is one thing about us that never changes. We have need of love as a fish has need of water, as a bird has need of air. We are not like the cold people of the North, who can dispense with love because they love themselves so much. We need the security of the family, the warmth of a wife, the passion of a lover. Without it, we become warped and twisted, like tropical trees transplanted to the snow fields. In the child, this need is doubled. He is born of an act of love. He is nursed at the breasts of love. If he is to grow, he must feed on love as a plant feeds on the soft spring rains."

He pulled a chair towards him and straddled it, leaning his arms and his chin on the frame of the back.

"Now, my friend, let me tell you the first thing I learned about the scugnizzi. Every one of them had left home because there was no longer any love for him. Does that seem strange to you?"

Yes, it did seem strange. It was too simple, too pat, to explain the complicated end product which is the scugnizzo. I said as much to Borrelli. He shook his head, vigorously.

"It is true, believe me. The circumstances vary but the essential fact remains. Consider a moment how it happens. In this family there are too many children and too little bread. The father is absent all day and the mother has so many cares that her love dries up as her milk does. In the next house there is jealousy and dissension. The mother has a lover, or the father has. There are quarrels and angry scenes, unendurable to the child, who is again cheated of love. Here there is misery so great that the child must work to bring in a few hundred lire. To his employer he is cheap labour. To his family, he is a breadwinner. None spares a thought for his starved little heart which dries out and withers like a walnut. Look again and you will see a house

94

in which the family life is poisoned by the guilt of incest and promiscuity. A girl has children by her father or her brother; love cannot last in such a climate. So, one day, the child leaves home where there is no love and joins the other loveless in the streets of the city."

"And does he find love there?"

Don Borrelli nodded, soberly.

"Sometimes, yes. The scugnizzi know how to be kind to one another, at least to members of their own band. The older ones protect the younger. When one is sick, the others will find extra food for him. They will steal medicines and give him clothes from their own backs. They are loyal to each other and will suffer much before they will betray one another. Sometimes there is even an element of love when a street woman takes a scugnizzo into her house and comforts him with her own body." He paused a moment and, when he spoke again, his voice was heavy with sadness. "But, you see, it is never enough. The human heart is a bottomless well and these are cupfuls poured into it only to be soaked up by the arid earth."

He stood up, suddenly, and thrust the chair away from him. His finger stabbed at me like a scalpel.

"Now! Now, I will show you how a scugnizzo is made. The foundation of his normal life is destroyed. He must build another for himself. He becomes vain and boastful, because there is no love to affirm his real value as a son of a family, as a son of God. He becomes cunning, because there is no love to protect him from the malice of others. There is only himself, the animal. He cheats and lies because honesty would make him the prey of those who have no love in their heart. He becomes nervous, raucous, unstable, because his child's body cannot keep pace with this explosive psychological development. His body becomes stunted as you have seen, while his mind spreads itself in rank and twisted growth like a weed on a dunghill. Sometimes he is a little mad. Sometimes . . ." Borrelli's face darkened. "Sometimes the burden of life becomes too much for him and he commits suicide."

He put his hands up to his face and pressed the palms into his eyeballs as if to blot out a terrifying vision. Then he calmed a little and went on:

"When I went on the streets, I was a man. More than this, I was a priest with years of discipline and study behind me. But I tell you, truly, even I was affected by this naked, loveless existence. When I stood outside the tourist hotels and pleaded to carry a bag, I hated the well-fed smiling men and the women whose clothes would feed a scugnizzo for more than a year. When I saw the police with their truncheons and their little black pistols, I wanted to spit on them and hammer their faces with my fists. Could they not see our wretchedness? Were we not human as they were? What right had they to thrust us out of their way as if we were animals and they a special creation of the Almighty? I knew my hatred was wrong. I knew I had to control it or fall into grievous sin. But the children? How could they understand? Cheated of love and faith, what was left to them but the luxury of hate?"

Abruptly the passion was quenched in him like a candle and I saw before me a weary young man with a pale face and sad eyes, and behind him a desk littered with documents and unpaid bills. He read my thoughts, and grinned, wryly.

"We get by, as the Americans say. But there is so much to do, and so little help to do it."

I left him then, because I had an appointment in the Hotel Vesuvio with an American friend who wanted to sell me a car. As I mounted the steps a pair of grubby urchins tugged at my coat-tails.

Don Mario Borrelli

Naples on Friday, the
traditional washing day

The sleep of the homeless and hungry

Children of Naples

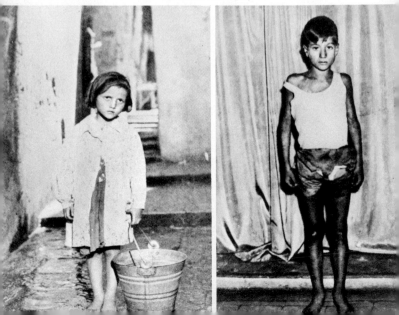

Borrelli with two friends who are shy of the police

The Salvation Army at work. Borrelli is in the cloth cap

Stolen boots on a
sleeping *scugnizzo*

There is food, but
prices are high

"Dollar, Joe! Dollar! You got cigarettes?"

The doorman tried to hunt them away. He thought I was a fool when I gave them a fresh packet of cigarettes and a thousand-lire bill. I probably was. If a tourist wants any peace in Naples, he must harden his heart and button his pockets.

When I remembered what I had heard from Don Borrelli, I found I could do neither.

*   *   *

The longer Borrelli lived with the scugnizzi, the more he understood that the house he hoped to build for them would have to be of a very special kind.

These were a special kind of children—half men, half boys. To pen them in an institution would be an intolerable cruelty. They would stifle with fear or burst into a frenzy of revolt. To submit them to the discipline of a classroom and a timetable, would be to make another torment for their distraught little souls. To lecture them on religion and morals and citizenship would be like talking to them in a foreign language.

What then? Where to begin and how?

Watching them at night huddled over their little fire, their skinny bodies shivering with cold, their pinched faces intent on a card game or the tally of the day's takings, he saw that the first things he must give them were food and shelter. He must cram their shrunken bellies with pasta and put a roof over their heads and give them a blanket to keep out the cold.

He must make a place to which they would return willingly, because it was better than anything they could find in the streets. He must give them security with freedom and food without a price ticket. On the street they had found friendship and a small store of love. This he must

C.O.T.S.

not destroy but preserve, adding to it his own love and the abundant gentleness of his friend Spada, who was tramping the streets every day looking for a vacant place to house them. In bombed-out Naples, it was like chasing a will o' the wisp.

Later, he must get medical treatment for them—vitamin courses, anti-scorbutics, penicillin to treat the venereal diseases, which a few of them had caught from their contacts with the prostitutes.

Later still—much later—he must try to educate them and find places for them in the overcrowded, workless society of the Mezzogiorno. This education itself would present one of his most difficult problems.

How do you teach a child that the vices which have fed him and kept him alive are suddenly evil? How do you restore the ravaged innocence to which thieving and lying and prostitution and perversion have become a commonplace?

He looked at them again squatting over the dying warmth, and his heart was filled with pity for them and with anger against the injustice and selfishness which condemned them to this vagabond animal life. They were children, all of them, even those of sixteen and seventeen. The street had consumed their bodies, stunting them to the stature of the old Spanish dwarfs. The younger ones looked like nursling children. Even their names were diminutive—Carlucciello, Tonino, Peppino.

As he watched them, one of the little ones began to tremble violently. His teeth chattered and he tried to draw closer to the tin dish full of coals. Borrelli moved forward and bent over him.

"*Cos' è Nino?* What's the matter?"

The tiny simian face looked up at him. The dark eyes were full of tears, but Nino was too much of a man to cry.

"I'm cold, Mario. I'm cold."

Borrelli lifted him in his arms and sat back in the angle of the wall, cradling the wasted body in his arms. Suddenly the child was wrenched with a spasm of coughing. His tiny chest caved in, his belly muscles knotted, then he vomited on the pavement. The priest wiped the boy's mouth with his hand—a handkerchief is a unbelievable luxury among the urchins—then he looked down at the vomit. It was mucous, dark and clotted and stained with little gouts of blood. Nino was in an advanced stage of tuberculosis.

Blind rage took hold of the priest and he cursed this dark city that crucified its children or shouldered them off its sidewalks to cough their hearts out in a gutter. Then the rage left him and he prayed—prayed for the courage and the strength and the wisdom to lead these lost ones out of the desert into a place of rest and refreshment. And, as he prayed, he held the sick child against his breast, trying to warm him with his own body, while all the time the bleak wind stirred along the alleys and the thin brown cats prowled among the rubbish heaps.

All the time the others watched him, their wary eyes full of dumb admiration. They were glad to have this Mario in their band. He gave them courage and a sense of security. He was different from the others, though they had no words to describe the difference.

How could they? Mario Borrelli had brought love to the children of the streets, but the word itself was still a strangeness and a mockery.

*　　*　　*

The next day, Borrelli slipped away from the boys on the pretext of scrounging medicine for the sick Nino. He had contacts to make. First with Spada to tell him that he could wait no longer and that, willy-nilly, a house must be found for the boys, even if they had to camp them in the court-yard of the Cardinal's palace; then with the journalist-photographer, whose help he needed to stage-manage the critical moment of his revelation as a priest.

Spada had good news for him. He had found a place—not much of a place to be sure, but it had a roof and stout walls and plenty of space. It had been damaged by bombs and it needed a lot of cleaning up. No matter! Eagerly Borrelli went off with his friend. The place was in a tiny square in the centre of a tangle of alleys at the back of the Via Teresa.

It was an abandoned church, dedicated in the old days to the Mother of God. That was its Latin name, Materdei. Like most Neapolitan churches it was in the baroque style with a high cupola and a circular apse and an ambulatory round the dome. It was filled with dirt and rubbish, but, as Spada said, it had a roof and stout walls. Cardinal Ascalesi was prepared to turn it over as shelter for the boys.

Ebbene! It was a beginning. The place was cold and empty as a tomb, but after the streets and the reeking lanes it was a paradise.

Borrelli's eyes shone. Now Spada must go out and beg, borrow or steal jute sacking and straw to make mattresses. If he could come by a few blankets, all the better. Next a cook pot and a pan and whatever food he could lay his hands on. Mountains of pasta they would need, anything else he could squeeze or threaten out of the shopkeepers. Medicines, too, if he could lay his hands on them.

What sort of medicines? Anything—everything! The needs of the boys were so great that almost anything in the pharmacopoeia could be useful. What they didn't need they could sell, and buy other things.

Spada grinned at his friend's enthusiasm. Then he pre-sented him with a sobering thought. Even today he does the same thing. Borrelli is an enthusiast, a thruster, a battler. He consumes his strength in the endless battle to keep his work and his boys alive. Spada is the counsellor, the calm one, the loving one, who looks after his friend as he looks after the boys, keeping the house running and the fires stoked. The question he put was of startling simplicity.

"We bring the boys here—good. We give them sleeping room, food and medicine—better still. But how do we keep them fed? How do we make a home for them? We have nothing, literally nothing, but four walls."

Mario Borrelli bunched his small fist and rubbed it against Spada's unshaven chin in an affectionate gesture. His wide mouth split into a grin. Not for nothing had he been a scugnizzo! There were more ways of killing a cat than by stuffing it with red peppers! There were a dozen flea markets in Naples where you could sell old clothes and scrap iron. He would organise a house to house collection for saleable rubbish. He would go to the Americans and point out that it was better to keep the boys off the street than have them pestering Allied troops and getting the Joes into bother. He would have his journalist friend publish some of the photographs and use them as a lever to prise money from the tight-fisted Neapolitans. Don't worry! He had learnt a lot about the little 'combinations' by which the urchins lived. He would clean them up and turn them into honest traffic. Let Spada not worry too much about the future. That was God's business. Their business was to get started.

Spada smiled affectionately. Even if he was only half-convinced he did not say so. *Allora!* He would start work at his end. When did Mario expect to bring the boys in?

Borrelli's face clouded. That was a horse of a different colour. He was still afraid of that menacing moment of revelation. If he mistimed it, if he had overrated his influence with the scugnizzi, his work would be wrecked in less than a minute. He would have to stage it carefully. He had certain ideas, but he could not be sure. He was worried.

Now it was Spada's turn to give encouragement and hope.

The work, he pointed out, was not their work but God's. He cocked a quizzical eye at Mario Borrelli and quoted scripture: "Unless the Lord build the house, they labour in vain that build it." It was necessary to be careful, to use tact and judgment and the Neapolitan sense of theatre—*sicuro*! But after that, it was up to the Almighty.

True enough! Borrelli chuckled ruefully and conceded the point. They talked a little longer, then, leaving Spada to his mountainous logistics, Borrelli took himself off to an appointment with his journalist friend in the Galleria Umberto.

His problem was a curious one.

Italy is a Catholic country. The faith is deeply rooted in the hearts of its people, most deeply here in the South. Nonetheless, Italy is the most violently anti-clerical country in Europe. For a variety of reasons, some of them already noticed in this book, there is a deep cleavage between the body of believers and their pastors. There is a dichotomy of conscience which is strange and disturbing to a Catholic from abroad who, good or bad, accepts as an elementary truth the participation of the clergy in social activity and civic reform. The priest is accepted as a man. The man is accepted as a priest. Here in the Mezzogiorno it is not so.

This was Borrelli's dilemma. When he informed the scugnizzi that he was a priest, they would not believe him. If he appeared among them in his soutane and his black platter hat, they would not believe he was the same man. He might look the same, but he would not be the same. It would be another trick, and they would edge away from him in fear and distrust.

Hence the need of the photographer. Borrelli would give him a list of the meeting places of his little band of scugnizzi. He would give him an approximate timetable. Then he must go round with his camera and flashbulb and take pictures of the boys, and of Borrelli too sharing their activities and their food and their sleeping places. He would develop the shots and give the prints to Borrelli who would use them as exhibits when he faced the critical court of the scugnizzi to establish his faith and his good will. Later, the same pictures could be used to publicise the work and bludgeon the Neapolitans out of their selfishness and their indifference.

So it was done. It took the best part of a week, because the scugnizzi were always on the move—away from the police, towards a new and more profitable stamping-ground. But, finally, the pictures were ready. Once more Borrelli slipped away from his band to prepare himself for the great moment of revelation.

He conferred with Spada and went with him to the old church to see that everything was ready. What he saw pleased him, and Spada's gentle face lit up with pathetic pride in his handiwork.

On the cold tiles of the ancient apse, there was a row of old sacks filled with sweet new straw. Each sack had a grey blanket, thin and threadbare. There was a rough table and one chair. There was a small pile of firewood. Best of all there was a gunnysack full of macaroni and a can of tomato paste. There were cook pots and a pile of rusty tin dishes and a few forks and spoons that had seen better days.

The two priests looked at one another and smiled wanly.

It wasn't much, but it was a beginning. The stable was ready for the Christ-children of the bassi.

Borrelli's shoulders shook. Spada put a gentle arm round his shoulders and led him across the apse to the altar, empty now and despoiled of its ancient glory. Together they knelt on the sanctuary steps and prayed, and the love that flowed out from them warmed the cold stones of the Church of the Mother of God.

* * *

It was late at night when Mario Borrelli went back to the scugnizzi. He had chosen this time because it was the worst time of all in the life of the urchin. The sun was gone. The commerce of the day with its thrills and triumphs and dangers was finished. The last guests were trickling out of the casinos, the theatre crowds were long since gone. The tourists were sleeping in their beds and the last jolly-boats had gone with the last load of drunken sailors. The boys would be alone again, huddling over the last pitiful coals, and when the fire died the cold and the darkness would eat into their bones and into their hearts. He knew how they felt, wretched, isolated, lost. He had felt so, himself.

He had stripped off his urchin's rags and dressed himself in his priestly black. In his breast pocket was the small sheaf of photographs, the proof of his good faith. He walked slowly through the dark lanes of the bassi, praying a little, fearing much. A life's work depended on the outcome of the next ten minutes.

He turned one corner, then another. He passed an ancient fountain carved with the arms of a forgotten prince. He skirted the blind wall of a church and passed a dark, evil-smelling archway. He turned into a narrow lane that opened off the alley. It was a cul-de-sac. At the end of it, just settling themselves for sleep, were the boys of his band.

They looked up when they heard his footfall, and when they saw that he was a priest, they cowered back, blank-faced and staring like small frightened animals. He took off his hat and stood looking down at them.

He grinned, cheerfully, and asked them in dialect:

"Don't you remember me? Mario?"

They stared at him with dumb hostility. He took a torch out of his pocket and shone it on his stubbly face.

"Look! It's really me. You know me, don't you? You, Carlucciello? You, Tonino? You, Mozzo?"

At the sound of their names they started and stared at one another in disbelief. Carlucciello heaved himself to his feet, lounged over to him and stared insolently into his eyes. Nino, the sick one, coughed and spat and groaned unhappily. Then Carlucciello spoke:

"You look like Mario, sure. But you're not. What do you want here? Why don't you get back to your convent?"

The boys tittered uneasily. Carlucciello was a real guappo. He knew how to handle the priests. Borrelli grinned and fished in his pockets for the bunch of photographs. He fanned them out and handed them to Carlucciello.

"First I want to show you that I really am Mario. Go on! Take a look at those. Use the torch if you want to."

Carlucciello took the torch and then, squatting, shone it on the photographs while the others crowded round, chattering uneasily and looking from the glossy prints to the white face of the priest standing above them. Borrelli talked, too.

"You remember now, don't you? That's the one that was taken the night after we met the sailors outside Filomena's place. That's the one where we were eating chocolate that Mozzo pinched from the American car. That's the one where Nino was sick and he was sleeping in my arms all night. You know me, don't you, Nino? I got the medicines for you, didn't I, and the big pills that made you feel better?"

The small wasted child looked up at him.

"It's Mario all right. How would he know all these things, if he was someone else?"

Carlucciello stood up again. His eyes were hostile. He handed back the prints and the torch without a word. Then, after a long minute, he spoke. His voice was quiet and angry and the little group shifted uneasily.

"All right, Mario, what's the game? Yesterday you were one of us, today you're a black crow. What's the story?"

"The story comes later, Carlucciello. I'm a priest, sure. Why and how I'll tell you later. Right now I've come to tell you that I found a place for us—it's not much, but there are beds and blankets and a fire and food. It was the best I could do. Nino's sick. If he stays on the streets, he'll die. I'd like you to come and have a look. If it doesn't please you, you can leave. It's your place, not mine."

Carlucciello's dark face was twisted with anger and contempt. He had trusted this fellow like a brother and now he turned out to be a dirty priest. Carefully, he filled his mouth with spittle then voided it full in the face of Mario Borrelli. Then he threw back his head and laughed. The sound echoed horribly along the empty lane.

The other boys watched in tense amazement. These were the leaders. Of the two Mario was closer to them, but not this way, not in this hated garb of authority. They watched to see what he would do.

Carefully Borrelli wiped the spittle from his face. He shoved the torch into his pocket and, still holding the prints in his hand, squatted down against the wall, heedless of the mud and filth that soiled his black cassock.

When he spoke, his voice was quiet and controlled.

"If you'd done that to me yesterday, Carlucciello, I'd have broken your nose and you know it. I could still do it. You know that, too. But I've let you have your fun. Now sit down here and listen. If you don't like what I say, you can go away. It doesn't matter. But you've got to listen. Is that fair or isn't it?"

The boys nodded and whispered among themselves. This was Mario all right. That was the way he used to talk —quietly, easily; and what he said, he did. They hesitated a moment then squatted beside him. Borrelli took Nino in his arms and cradled him against his breast in the old way. After a moment Carlucciello squatted again, but a little apart. He would listen, sure. But he was too wise to be taken in by shabby tricks like this one.

Borrelli sat a moment in silence, considering his words. They had to be the right words, or the boys would race away from him and he would never come near them again. He said, simply:

"I know what you're thinking: that I want to take you into an orphanage where they close the gates and send you to school and read lectures at you and let you out to walk in a crocodile on Sundays." He grinned cheerfully. "I couldn't do that even if I wanted to. This place I've got isn't much, but it keeps the rain out. There's straw for you to sleep on and a blanket apiece. There's wood for a fire and enough food to give you a good meal. You can stay there the night and leave in the morning. If you like it, you can come back again, any time, for a feed and a bed. It's better than the street, isn't it?"

The boys nodded, silently. They looked at Carlucciello, but he was staring at the ground drawing a dirty picture in the mud with his finger.

Borrelli went on:

"I'm going there now. I don't want to force you to come. You can follow me or stay here, just as you want. The only thing is, I'm carrying Nino. It's a long way and he's sick. I'm going to try to get a doctor and medicine for him. That's all. From here on, it's up to you."

Abruptly he stood up, hoisted Nino on to his shoulders and carried him pick-a-back down the dark alley. He heard the whispers and the scuffling but he did not look back. He plodded onwards, head down, arms behind his back supporting the puny child who clung to his shoulders like a monkey.

It was not until he reached the Via San Gennaro that he dared to look behind.

The boys were a dozen yards away, padding along his tracks. A long, long way behind, but still following, was the skinny stooping figure of Carlucciello.

His heart leapt. His mouth split into a grin as wide as a water melon and he started to whistle the jaunty little tune of the 'Duckling and the Poppy-flower'.

The Pied Piper of Naples was bringing his children home.

CHAPTER SEVEN

THE FIRST thing that strikes the visitor to the House of the Urchins is its poverty. This poverty is a daily indictment of the selfishness and social indifference of wealthy Italians. Here are two young men keeping 110 homeless boys and ten paid helpers for less than a dollar a day each. Try it yourself and see if you like the taste of it—a dollar a day for food, clothing, housing, light, water, gas, electricity and medical services, to say nothing of education, textbooks and all the thousand contingencies of a charitable organisation.

The place looks poor. It is an old grey building in a back street and it looks out on rows of tenements with washing strung from the balconies and chickens pecking among the dust heaps. There are bedrooms with rows of chipped iron cots, each with two blankets and a pair of unbleached sheets and a tiny towel.

There is a small dispensary where the senior boys adminster first aid. There are a couple of classrooms and a dining room and a small kitchen with a cooking range but no refrigerator. There is a bathroom with a cold shower and a row of hand-and-foot basins but no hot water. No gentleman of Naples has yet thought to donate a storage system.

There is a long narrow room with a television set where the youngsters sit entranced every evening at five-thirty. There is a pocket-handkerchief yard at the back of the Church, bought with a papal grant of 5,000,000 lire. It looks a lot when you say it in lire, but it's less than 3000 English pounds.

The boys' food is rough but plentiful—pasta with the inevitable tomato sauce, meat once a week, soup, bread and jam, occasional fruit. If you care to turn back to the cost of living figures in the second chapter of this book, you'll see why there isn't much variety. You'll also wonder how they manage so well on a dollar a day per person. The boys' clothes are poor and patched, but warm and serviceable. They don't wear uniforms, they can't afford them. But when the older ones go to work they buy themselves a suit, and when the young ones go to school each has a clean smock so that he is indistinguishable from all the others of his class.

When Padre Spada takes you round on a tour of inspection, you sense the diffidence and the pathetic pride as he tells you how much has been done and with how little. There is a small grant from the funds of a papal organisation. There is no help at all from the Government or the *Comune*. Most of it has been paid for by the sale of scrap iron and old clothes and by a trickle of private charity, sporadic and uncertain like all good works in Naples.

The place is clean and the boys are clean, in a rough and ready sort of way. The building is centuries old. The plaster cracks off and the tufa walls shed a fine grey dust that settles on everything. The boys play in an unpaved courtyard between the high walls of crumbling tenements.

Yet they are happy. They are free to walk out at any time. They stay because they want to stay, because they have found a warmth and a love stronger even than the call of the streets. They are proud of themselves and of their house, and this pride is the more striking for the poverty in which it flourishes.

It is little, you say, pitifully little after five years' heartbreak and sacrifice. True. But when you think of the ruinous beginning and the rank indifference of the gentry of Naples, it is a very great thing indeed.

The first bunch of uneasy urchins who came to the Materdei for food and straw beds, left the following morning. Mario Borrelli made no move to stop them. He gave them breakfast on the night's leftovers, stuffed a few cigarettes in their tattered pockets and told them the place would be open all night and all day for any who cared to come. He told them something else, too. If any of them were picked up by the police, the others were to bring him a message and he would bail out the offender. The boys grinned uneasily. The thought was new to them but it might turn out useful. They bade him an offhand farewell and trotted off to the day's trading in the bassi.

The next night they were back again, with a few more tattered recruits. The cook pot was bubbling and the warm blankets were inviting. The new arrivals had to double up on the straw mattresses. While they ate, Borrelli leaned against the wall and played them music on his battered accordion. There were no prayers, no lectures, only a warm diffusion of love and companionship. Borrelli is an impatient man, but the urchin life had taught him that the leaven of goodness works very, very slowly.

So they came and went and when they learnt that there was no compulsion, no hidden trickery, they stayed a little longer. Borrelli and Spada profited by the respite to add a few more comforts—a chair or two, a bed for the sick ones, an old stove, cast-off jackets and battered shoes begged from the poor. They had discreet talks with the questura to whom the boys were as troublesome as March flies. Instead of hustling them off to a house of correction, why not bring them to the Materdei and give Borrelli a chance to straighten them out?

The police were sceptical. The boys were tough little criminals. A priest was hardly equipped to handle them. Borrelli fished out his photographs and talked with passion and conviction. He, too, could be tough when he wanted to and he was not above using his knowledge of certain police peccadilloes to win his point. The questura began to see some reason in his views.

Then, one night, after the food and the music, Borrelli squatted on the floor in the centre of the circle of mattresses and laid down his proposition. His speech was couched in the vivid argot of the streets.

He had done what he promised to do. Right? He had

given them food and shelter without questions and without price tickets. Right?

Right! The boys nodded agreement.

They trusted him?

Sicuro!

They knew that he didn't play tricks or talk with two tongues?

Sicuro, again.

Now, they agreed that he knew a thing or two about earning a crust?

The boys grinned and giggled. They knew all right. He was a guappo, this one. They had seen him work.

Fine! Now this was his idea. Instead of working the streets the way they did now, instead of having to run from the police and the carabinieri, instead of having to scavenge in the filth of the lanes and be pushed about by shopkeepers and hotel porters, why not work together? Why not make a home here and organise their own trade? They could do it in the daytime and have their nights free.

"What sort of trade?" Carlucciello asked the question, but Borrelli knew it was in the minds of the others as well.

He explained, simply:

"What do you do now, you, Carlucciello, or you, Peppi? You steal *stracci* (old clothes) or car batteries or spare parts or carpenters' tools. Then you sell them in the flea market up in Pugliano or in Porticino. Check?"

"Check."

"Good. You do the same thing now. Only you make it legal. You earn the same money as you do now, probably better, because you won't be in trouble with the police and the fences won't be able to beat you down because you won't be scared. You see?"

Carlucciello nodded. He saw everything, except where his stock was coming from.

Borrelli explained that, too. He would beg some of it, buy the rest. He knew how to bargain. He would get it at a good price. Then, they would clean it up and sell it at a profit. How did that sound?

The boys nodded eagerly. Even Carlucciello was impressed.

Borrelli was a wise man, and his wisdom was tempered with Southern shrewdness. He knew that he was appealing to one of the deepest desires of the scugnizzo, indeed of every Neapolitan male—the desire for respectability and a secure place in society. This thwarted desire produces the vanity, the cocky self-assertion which are the most irritating traits of the Southerner.

He was also appealing to their *furberia*, the instinct for trade and a sharp bargain. He waited; the boys waited too, watching for a lead from Carlucciello. The dark fellow was framing another question.

"It sounds fine so far. But if it doesn't work out, we call it off, eh? We can quit whenever we like?"

"Whenever you like."

"*D'accordo!*" said Carlucciello, briskly. "It's a deal. When do we start?"

"Tomorrow," grinned Mario Borrelli. He picked up his accordion, slung the strap over his shoulder and broke into a familiar Neapolitan song, '*Scaptriciatiello*'. The boys joined in with high raucous voices and the sound echoed round and round the cracked plaster of the dome.

*   *   *

That night was the real beginning of the House of the Urchins as it exists today. At one stroke, Borrelli had brought off a number of critical operations.

He had turned the Materdei from a soup kitchen into a home. He had turned the first scugnizzi from rogues and vagabonds into independent traders. He had established a small source of income for their upkeep. He had enabled the older ones like Carlucciello to qualify for work cards as street vendors or as collaborators of a charitable institution. He had something to show to Cardinal Ascalesi and the civil authorities when he asked for assistance to consolidate and develop the work. Now, when he went round the streets picking up the strays from under the barrows or over the bakers' gratings, he could promise them companionship and understanding as well as a bed and a meal. With Spada as administrator and father of the household, he could begin the slow and devious process of re-education.

This, it seemed to me, was the most critical point of my investigation. By this the work of Borrelli and Spada must stand or fall. For all the drama of its beginning, for all the warm charity that pervades it, the only measure of its value is its success or failure in the re-education of the scugnizzi and their integration into normal life.

I said as much to Don Borrelli. He agreed, wholeheartedly. I told him I wanted freedom to investigate for myself. He told me I could ask any questions I wanted. Both he and Spada would answer them frankly. I told him this wasn't enough. The clerical point of view might not convey the whole truth. This book must be an honest one, else it were better left unwritten. I, myself, had been a teacher in elementary and high schools for nearly ten years. I wanted to move among the boys. I wanted to question them freely. I wanted to associate with the elder ones, go out with them into the city, revisit the scenes of their old activities, study their reactions, make my own summing-up of the success or failure of the Casa.

Borrelli grinned cheerfully and told me I could do as I pleased. He gave me a bed in the infirmary and the freedom of the house. What I tell you here is my own finding. I assure you I have not written it lightly.

* * *

The first thing I noticed was an odd one.

Every boy who came to the House of the Urchins—whether the police brought him, or Borrelli, or whether he drifted in himself—left it again within three or four days. The new life was so strange, the call of the streets was so strong, that his puzzled, restless little mind couldn't support the strain. He ran away. The porter would see him go, some of the boys, perhaps, but nobody made any move to stop him. It is the rule of the house—the door opens both ways. The Casa exists for the boys, not the boys for the Casa. It is their home: if they don't want to stay there, if the love it offers is not enough, they are free to go.

But they always come back. Three days, four days, a week later, a small tousled head and a grubby face pokes uncertainly round the door. Can he have a meal or watch the television? Sure! The porter or the monitor jerks a thumb upstairs. He knows where to go. It's all open! The thin urchin figure scuttles past the door and heads uncertainly towards the kitchen or the playground or the classroom. If Padre Spada meets him in the corridor, he rumples the tousled head and smiles cheerfully.

"Don't forget to wash yourself before you go to bed."

It's as easy as that. Nobody asks questions. It is enough that the boy is home again.

Some of them have left the Casa two or three times. These, too, have come back, generally escorted by a policeman. The reason is a curious one, and it has its own peculiar pathos. The boy has lived in the Casa. He has dropped his guard. He has not the same need of cunning and hard-headed cynicism. When he returns to the streets, he is out of practice. He cannot survive like the others.

Back in the Casa, he begins to change, little by little. The fear goes out of his eyes. He loses the furtive, uneasy look of the hunted. He is no longer strident and assertive. He grins when you talk to him. He starts to play in the court-yard. His body starts to grow visibly, he fills out and shoots up like a bamboo stalk in the tropics. I've seen it with my own eyes and it is a moving experience.

It took me a little time to understand the true nature of the phenomenon. The scugnizzo is returning to his natural state—an untroubled childhood, free of the scarifying re-sponsibilities of survival. He does not have to worry about food or money or a place to sleep. He is not troubled by the guilt of his actions or by the fearful presence of the law. The people about him are friendly. The love that is offered has the cheerful indifference of family affection. So the spirit becomes tranquil and his stunted body starts to grow. But it will never grow like the body of your child or mine, because the love and the care have come too late.

*　　*　　*

"What about the past? Does the child forget?"

I put the question to Padre Spada as we stood one even-ing in a corner of the small playground, watching the youngsters booting a soccer ball. They looked like any bunch of healthy, grubby kids in any vacant lot. Spada rubbed his chin and peered at me through his thick spec-tacles. His voice was gentle and reflective.

"We try to make them forget. I think we succeed in part with the young ones. When they come to us first they have nightmares. They grind their teeth and mutter in their sleep. Sometimes they wake screaming. Later they sleep quietly. They forget because they want to forget. Though we all know that, even when we forget, we do not destroy a memory."

"Do they forget their vices, too? Those who have had contact with street women by the time they are ten? Those who have been taken by the pederasti? Do they bring their vices into the Casa?"

His answer to that one was frank and interesting.

"In general, the answer is no. I think we have less trouble here with sexual aberrations than you would find in any fashionable boarding school for boys of good family. There is a reason for it. The early contacts with women of the street are unsatisfactory to an unformed boy. They take place in circumstances which damage his self-respect. The desire which they arouse in him consumes his frail strength. In a curious fashion he understands that. When he is removed from the occasion, he is unconsciously glad of it. His interests here—the games, the school, the life of the Casa—are much more satisfactory to him than to a boy who has had them all his life. Therefore he is not, for the present at least, interested to renew his contacts with women."

"And the other thing—homosexual contact?"

"We have found occasional offenders, but not many."

"Any reason? The normal experience is that pederasty is a difficult habit to eradicate."

Spada nodded:

"As a normal experience, yes. But again you must understand the scugnizzo is not a normal delinquent. When he comes here for the first time, he is likely to do anything. He will lie, cheat, fight. He will try to find somebody with whom to share his vice. It is his form of revolt, you see. But when he comes back, after his first flight, it is because he has realised that here he is more a man, more his own man, than he is on the streets. So he develops a sharp reaction against pederasty."

"A moral reaction?"

"No. A very natural one. He understands in his own way that to give oneself to another boy is to put himself in the power of that boy. He has had that experience. He wants it no longer. Even for the pleasure, he will not do it. It is the streets that have taught him this elementary wisdom. What we try to do is to confirm it with our own moral teaching."

I liked the sound of that reasoning. It was simple, pragmatic and free from unctuous moralising. I thought it would appeal to any practising psychiatrist. Later I was to confirm its truth in long talks with Peppino and the senior boys of the Casa. For the present, I was content to leave it. There were other things I wanted to know.

"Cheating, for instance, lying, stealing? On your own showing the boys arrive as adepts in these things. Do they still practise them?"

Spada nodded.

"When they first come, yes. You must remember that the scugnizzo is an actor who has learned to wear the face he thinks will bring him most profit. The pleading face for the tourist. The knowing face for the sailors. The bargaining face for the fences and the pimps. When he comes here, he tries them all. It is often a long while before he understands that the only face we want to see is the real one—the face of the child."

This was something I had learned from my own experience. When I first came to the Casa with my pockets full of sweets for the young ones and cigarettes for the elders, I had been subjected to the same little comedy of wheedling and phony affection. After I had lived with them a while, they dropped it and treated me with the frank casualness of normal children.

118

"What about stealing?"

"No," said Spada, emphatically. "They are scugnizzi, they will not steal from their own. For the rest?" He shrugged comically. "We have so little here that is worth stealing, the question does not arise."

I left him then and went back to my little white room at the top of the Materdei to record our conversation and to collate it with the other facts I had collected on the humanising of the urchins.

* * *

For their formal education, the young ones are sent to a public elementary school, not far from the Casa. Each morning they are dressed in the black smocks which all Neapolitan children wear to school. Their faces are scrubbed and the ribbons tied at their necks and, after an inspection by one of the elder boys, they trot off together. There are still only two priests to run the Casa, and the hired helpers are concerned with cooking and cleaning and the second-hand trade which keeps the Casa going. So most of the teaching must be done outside.

This means that like most Neapolitan children the urchins get about three hours' schooling, three days a week. One relay goes from nine till eleven, the other from eleven to two, every second day. When they return to the Casa, the monitors help them with homework and conduct informal classes. It is an unsatisfactory situation, but it puts them on a par with the other children of Naples who are fortunate enough to have schools. In any case, they are much better off than those thousands who have none at all.

"How do they fare at school?"

I put the question to one of Borrelli's paid staff, a bright, intelligent youth from Calabria. He is paid 500 lire a day to act as monitor and assistant teacher. In workless Naples, he is glad to get it. More than this, as he explained simply, he feels that he is doing something useful for himself and for the children. He answered my question carefully.

"At school the boys do as all the others do. There is no distinction between the other pupils and the scugnizzi. They dress the same. The poor of Naples respect each other. If there is any advantage it is on the side of our boys. They are bright. The streets have made them so. More than this, when they come home, they are able to study a little and prepare their homework. The others, who live six, eight, twelve in a room in the bassi—how can they possibly study, even if they want to do so? *Capisce?*"

"*Capito.*" It was elementary but significant. It appeared that Borrelli and Spada were doing better than most with the limited means at their disposal.

By Anglo-Saxon standards, the achievement isn't great. The classrooms of the Casa are dusty and empty of teaching aids. There is a blackboard and a few tattered textbooks and a flyblown picture or two. And that's the list. But, when you see these youngsters bending over their homework with the monitors at their shoulders, you sense an eagerness and a hunger for knowledge that would shame some of our own children.

The House of the Urchins cannot afford to train its own teachers and force them through the state qualifying examinations. Even if it could, there would be no hope of paying them the statutory minimum on the modest income of a dollar a day per person. So the boys must do the best they can with the public schools, where the methods are of ancient vintage and where the overcrowding and the relay system break the heart of even the stoutest teacher.

When you look down on the waterfront of Naples, you see a fi. new square, which the mayor is building for his beloved citizens. The mayor is Mr Lauro and the square is right next to the handsome business offices of the Flotta

Lauro Company. Mr Lauro is a public-spirited man. He is the one who built a concrete wall in front of the hovels so they wouldn't spoil the drive along the Via Marittima. He has also presented the city with a magnificent new fountain. His latest gesture is the gift of a television set to every local branch of the Monarchist Party. I wonder why he hasn't thought of building a school or two for the children?

* * *

After the boy has been in the Casa awhile, a new problem presents itself—his parents or his relatives! Few of the boys are orphans. Most have some relative living in Naples. As Borrelli had explained to me often, as I have tried to explain in this book, it is not hunger or desertion or death that drives the boys out into the streets, it is the double burden of responsibility and a lack of love.

When the parent or the relative hears of the boy's good fortune in finding a home, his first reaction is to make a personal profit out of the situation.

A father will come, begging Borrelli to give him back his son. He loves him dearly. He cannot bear to be parted from him. He needs the child to help him in his business. A mother, who has seen her boy's photograph in the little broadsheet which Borrelli publishes, will present herself at the Casa asking payment. The neighbours have told her that photographic models have a right to be paid. She is the boy's mother, it is his duty to support her. When the boy goes home, as he sometimes does, to visit the family, they will work on him again, weeping, pleading, subjecting him, as they subject the tourist, to the contemptible little comedy of misery.

When, for instance, I suggested that we take a couple of the boys for a weekend in my house, Spada shook his head.

"Better not, my friend. It would be good for them, sure.

But when their families got to hear of it, you would be plagued by a stream of them demanding charity. We know how to deal with them. You don't."

The method of dealing with them is a blunt brutality. If they plague the boys too much, Borrelli threatens them with police proceedings for neglect of their children and breaches of the education and labour laws. He has fought too hard for his boys to allow them to be exploited again.

In spite of this, there is often a division of loyalty, which creates problems for the child himself. In the streets he was not aware of it. He had made his choice. He had to preserve his independence to live. In the Casa he drops his defence and he is again vulnerable to the venality of his family.

The atmosphere of the Casa is a free and easy one. No bells are rung. The boys are not assembled and marched from place to place as they are even in a normal boarding school. The older ones are allowed to smoke, not, as Spada explains, because it is good for them, but because they have become accustomed to the habit on the streets and it is as strong in them as it is in any adult. Better to allow them the luxury and have them feel at home than have them smoking in corners in a kind of small rebellion.

This liberal attitude is deliberately cultivated in the Casa and is specially important to the boys themselves. The first and most important thing in the minds of Borrelli and Spada is to give the boys a home. All else is secondary. If they feel themselves secure and free at the same time, they will settle down and re-educate themselves. They will act on their own responsibility to preserve their home and the principles on which it is founded.

When I saw the gentle care which the older ones lavished on the youngsters, when I saw Peppino's watchful eyes on the scugnizzi we met in our nightly wanderings in case any of the Casa boys had slipped back among them, I believed that Borrelli and Spada were right. Their methods were sound. Their success was obvious.

* * *

With the senior lads, those who have passed the five elementary grades and have reached say fifteen, sixteen or seventeen, a new problem presents itself. Rather, a series of problems, which even the rugged, combative genius of Borrelli cannot solve. To do so, he would have to topple down the whole political, economic and moral structure of the Mezzogiorno. Which mightn't be a bad idea. The drains are beginning to smell badly.

When his boys reach high school age, Mario Borrelli is faced with a simple but brutal choice. Does he educate them, or give them a chance to eat for a few years?

If he sends them to high school—which again he can't afford—they will be given a classical education in the old, old style. This education will open their minds to the best there is in literature, art, philosophy, history; and deny them for ever the means of enjoying it.

There are lawyers driving taxis in Naples. There are philosophers jerking espresso coffee. On every railway station you see notices advertising an examination for some minor civil service posts. The men who enter are Laureati in Arts, Law, Letters and Economics. One in a thousand has a chance of getting the job. For Borrelli's boys, therefore, this sort of education is a costly waste of time.

There is, of course, technical education. There's not much of it in Naples, but if you can enter one of the half a dozen colleges which offer it, you are lucky. Of course there are so few vacancies and so many parents ready to pay for the privilege, there's little hope for the scugnizzo.

Naturally, if any Neapolitan gentleman were to found a scholarship or two for the poor children of his city, the position would be different. Leaving aside this remote miracle, however, let's assume that Borrelli can get enough funds and enough influence to start a few of his boys on a technical course which will lead them with brains and hard work to, say, an agricultural diploma.

There is, in the South, an insidious system called *la raccomandazione*. To pass an examination and get class promotion and the final diploma, the student must not only get good marks, he must be *raccomandato*—recommended by his teacher. Since a technical diploma is one of the few passports to a job in Italy today, the teacher's recommendation is vitally important. You might even say it has a capital value.

That's what certain teachers say, too. They charge money for their recommendations. A friend of mine was asked, privately and discreetly, for 200,000 lire to recommend him for his engineering diploma. He didn't have the money. He wouldn't have paid it if he had. But it took him three more years to get the diploma—three years in which he might have been earning a technician's salary. What chance does an ex-scugnizzo have against a system like that?

So Borrelli takes the third and only road left to him. He apprentices his boys to tradesmen in the city—electricians, cabinet-makers, welders, engineers. The boys take kindly to their jobs. The life of the streets has made them conscious of the dignity of work and the good fortune of being able to get it.

I used to see them coming in at night, grimy, grease-stained, tired, to the small hostel which Borrelli found for them over by the Duomo. I used to eat with them and talk with them. They liked their jobs. They liked the feel of tools in their hands. They scrimped and saved to buy dog-eared technical magazines and handbooks. They were hungry to learn. But there was nobody to teach them!

It sounds crazy but it is true. There was nobody to teach them, because their employers did not want them to learn.

It staggered me at first, then I realised that I had stumbled on the explanation of something that had bothered me a long time.

Here in the South the standard of technical workmanship is terribly poor. I have stood for hours watching men working on a new villa. The cement was half-mixed, the courses were crooked, there were no flashings for window or door frames, there were no ventilators. The electrical wiring was a death-trap and the plumbing a mechanical monstrosity. Southern mechanics will shine your car to diamond brightness, but they are apt to tie the innards up with string.

The reason for it was explained to me by two of Don Borrelli's senior boys.

They were apprenticed at fifteen or sixteen. Their employers—a small cabinet-maker, a garage with six mechanics—taught them enough to do the odd jobs around the place. If they wanted to learn more, they were headed off to sweeping the floor or filtering sump oil. Why? First, if they learnt too much they could become potential rivals. Secondly, the employers had no intention of keeping them beyond their eighteenth year.

It is the old system, outlawed long since by sane business men in my country, of using up cheap labour and then tossing it back, half trained and helpless, in the unemployment pool.

Every one of the senior boys to whom I spoke, knew what was likely to happen to him. Every one of them was afraid. Doubly afraid, because he had no family to turn to when he lost his job.

Borrelli was afraid, too, afraid and angry, but he didn't know what he could do about it. He had talked to individual employers and had been met with the cocked head and the pitiful shrug. *Cosa fare?* Times were bad. It was a charity to take the boys in the first place, when there were tens of thousands of married men out of a job.

Biting back his anger, Borrelli would explain that to profit in this way from untrained youth, without assuming any obligation for their future welfare, was a grievous sin. It was sin of the same nature as profiting from the bodies of women in the closed houses. It destroyed human dignity. It . . .

Then he would break off, sickened by the bland indifference of these beggars on horseback. It angered him that he had to depend on these fellows to find work for his boys. But he had tried the big organisations and they could do little or nothing for him.

Top management was prepared to be co-operative, but the mechanics of the operation brought Borrelli finally to the door of the personnel manager. The answer was always the same. There were no vacancies. Naturally there can't be any vacancies in a city of two hundred thousand unemployed. Moreover it was the company's policy to give employment to married men. With that principle Borrelli could have no quarrel at all.

He might quarrel with the practice of certain personnel managers of collecting a small percentage from the men they hired. But where would it get him? Everybody in Naples plays the skin game!

And there he stands today, the man who has brought hope and love and human dignity to the homeless children of Naples. He has snatched them from the streets. He has given them a home, he has taught them to be honest, decent young men. He has educated them as best he can—and now? They must go back to the streets.

Why doesn't he train the boys himself, you ask? Why doesn't he set up a trade school and staff it with qualified teachers and make his own recommendations and feed Italian industry with the skilled technicians it so badly needs.

The answer is that he hasn't got the money and he can't get it. The funds of the Church are spread thinly over the many works of charity it has to support. Borrelli claims—I believe, honestly—that he is getting his fair share. From the State he gets nothing, yet these are the children of the State. From the Comune of Naples, nothing again, though these are the children of Naples, the lovable, romantic, sentimental city where the tourists come. From private charity he gets a small trickle of money, just enough to keep him in operation at his present standard.

He knows, as you and I know, that thousands of millions of American dollars have poured into this country to finance such works as this, to produce trained manpower to develop the resources of the depressed South. Italy is a poor country, they tell you. Its resources are meagre. True, but the resources could be tripled with honestly used money and trained personnel.

This year, the farmers of the South were crippled by the most rigorous winter in recent history. It was a disaster of the first magnitude. But I saw no fund created to assist the South. The Bank of Naples was still lending money at thirteen per cent and hoisting the rate to seventen per cent by discounting bonds. I have heard many disquieting stories of industrialists and bankers paying insurance money to Communist Party funds; but I have heard little of bequests and grants for relief of the widespread distress.

And the American dollars locked up in the Cassa del Mezzogiorno? The distressed farmers say they haven't seen any. They haven't been used to keep the price of olive oil down for workless families.

And certainly none of them has reached Don Mario Borrelli!

PART THREE

WHAT'S TO DO ABOUT IT?

CHAPTER EIGHT

THE FIRST thing that needs to be done is to answer a question.

By what right does a foreigner, a citizen of a country with full employment and a high standard of living, come to Italy, and sit in judgment on its social conditions and its political and ecclesiastical administration?

The question is a fair one. I think the answer is a fair one, too. The observer is invited to come. More money is spent by the Italian State on tourist advertising than on any charitable enterprise or social reform. The visitor pays a sojourn tax, and his living costs him a great deal more than it costs him in his own country for better food and better social standards. That, of course, is only a small part of the answer. Tourist revenue keeps this country afloat. Emigration to Australia, Canada, America and Argentina drains off at least a part of its workless population. United States dollars bolster its shaky industrial enterprises and provide cheap profits for its financiers and businessmen.

The man who pays the piper has some right to discuss the music offered to him.

More than this, with a tight bureaucracy, both in the State and in the Church, with a divided and partisan Press, financed, all of it, by sectional interests, the real truth is hard to come by. Yet we must have it.

Italy is the pivot of European defence, economic and military. Political corruption is a termite nest, chewing at the props of that defence. Social indifference breeds revolt among the victims of it. Misery and unemployment make good Communists. Venality in business and public life breeds fear and uncertainty and holds back reform. Rogues flourish and the voices of honest men are stifled.

No man is an island. No nation either, in this twentieth-century world. The sins of one are visited on the heads of all. The visitation may well be catastrophic.

There is my first justification for the writing of this book.

This the second: the children of Naples have no voice. I have pledged myself to give them one. A child has no politics. A child has no nationality. He has only the right to live, the right to hope. If these rights are denied him, it is a crime against humanity, and every honest man must raise his voice against it.

Just over the hills that front me as I write these lines lie the orchards and the tomato plots of Salerno. The fruit trees are in flower and the flowers grow out of the bodies that lie buried under the grey volcanic earth. They are the bodies of men who died believing that they were fighting for freedom from want and freedom from fear. The hunger and the fear that fester in the back streets of Naples are a daily mockery of their death. They, too, are voiceless. I speak for them also.

These are my credentials. By them I must stand for my right to say what ails this unhappy country and what must be done to mend it.

What must be done?

The needs are legion, but they all boil down to one: the cleansing of this country from administrative and political corruption, the formation of a social conscience, the creation of public confidence, an atmosphere of mutual trust, without which reform is impossible.

Put it like that, and it sounds like a piece of well-turned rhetoric. Let me show you what it really means.

*　　*　　*

I had been in Sorrento a few weeks when I began to be aware of the plight of the orange growers, whose trees had been burned by the frosts and who stood to lose more than half their crops. The olive orchards were in worse plight. The whole crop had been ruined and there was fear that the trees themselves might be killed. I live in orange country. I know a little about cultivation and more about the co-operative organisations of the growers. I knew for instance that the fabled orange trees of Sorrento were decades old and would have been rooted out long since by growers in Australia. This, by the way.

I noticed that tens of thousands of oranges fell every day and were left to rot on the ground. I noticed that the growers were leaving the rest of the fruit on the trees instead of picking and packing it. It was their primitive and wasteful method of keeping the price up. It didn't work, of course, because the daily losses outweighed the price rise. The fruit that was left was over-ripe and of poor quality. I looked in vain for nurseries of young trees to replace the ones which would die and never bear again. I saw none.

Then, for my own edification, I began to canvass the idea of a local co-operative to control marketing, to set up packing sheds and cool storage, to negotiate with the bank for loans at a reasonable rate, to finance new plantings and provide sinking funds against bad times like this one.

Everyone to whom I spoke agreed that it was a good

idea. Many were well-informed on the operation of rural co-operatives in Denmark, in America and other countries. Not one gave the scheme half a chance of success in Sorrento.

Why?

Nobody trusted anybody else. The history of corporate enterprise in Italy in the last twenty years was a history of speculation and scandal. The honest men with organising ability wouldn't commit themselves to a new effort. The farmers preferred to keep their funds under their own hands, stuffed in the mattress or behind the loose brick in the wall of the living room.

And there you have it—administrative corruption, the lack of social conscience. It was the story of my journalist friends all over again. The plot was the same, only the sets were different.

More than this, when I asked—more for a test exercise than from any hope of success—for permission to enter the orchards and pick up the fallen fruit, and cart it, at my own expense, to the House of the Urchins, I was refused. I might buy it at half the price of good fruit. If I wasn't prepared to buy it, it would rot on the ground. Two days later I watched them digging it in. The real reason was not meanness, but a fear that I might take the fruit and sell it for my own profit!

Fiducia! Trust! Mutual confidence! Any business man will tell you that it is the only foundation of a prosperous and stable economy. Unless, of course, he's an Italian of the Mezzogiorno!

How do you start reforms in an atmosphere like this? The obvious answer is that you must start with education. In Anglo-Saxon countries, it is still possible to start press campaigns on issues of public importance—road deaths, cancer research, the needs of the aged. Our own Press can be partisan enough, God knows, but there are certain matters on which opinion is united. In Italy, no. I proved this one, too, by personal experience.

Two papers in the South had asked me to write some material for them. I had refused. My reason was that I did not care to damage my credit as an independent observer by publishing in any paper whose political affiliations I could not check. However, after the episode of the orange growers I made contact with the editors concerned and offered to write the story as a public service, with emphasis on the value of such co-operatives to the rural economy of the South. Both declined. One of them was frank enough to tell me that he couldn't get the story past his management.

With the channels of communication turned into party lines, how do you begin to spread the truth and preach reform? The most obvious answer is that reform must begin in Rome, that the public service must be purged and a campaign of re-education started from the top down.

The answer is obvious, but incomplete.

The fact is that Italy has been a nation for less than a hundred years. It is not a homogeneous country like Great Britain with a unified code of law and a tradition of public service. It is even less homogeneous than the United States which still has its own problems of State jurisdiction and is still divided on important issues like racial segregation.

The Italian administration is not a servant of the people, but its master, an instrument of control for the party in power. If you find this hard to believe, let me tell you another story. This one, too, is first-hand.

During our sojourn on the peninsula we employed a Sorrentine housemaid, a woman of thirty-nine. It was part of her contract of service that she should live in the house and, if she were given an evening off, she must return to the house before two in the morning. One evening she went to the pictures. She didn't return till breakfast time the next morning. When I questioned her, she dissolved into tears and told me that she had been afraid to return because she had gone to Piano di Sorrento, three townships away, to see a film and had forgotten her *documenti*—identity and employment cards. She was afraid to come home and had spent the night in the house of a friend.

I didn't see the point and I told her so with some heat. Then she explained. In Piano di Sorrento she was a stranger. If the police picked her up, as they were likely to do, and found she had no cards, she would have spent the night in the calaboose. No matter that they could check her identity by a telephone call to me. The point was that they wouldn't do it. In Piano she had no rights. The absence of papers proved that. Even when she showed her papers the next morning, she would have no redress against the arrest and imprisonment.

I checked this story with local residents. They grinned and told me it was true. It wouldn't happen to a tourist? Oh, no! Or to the local gentry? No, again. But to an unknown peasant? Sure!

There is a sheaf of such little tales of the public administration and its treatment of the tax-payers who support it, but why retail them? The facts are self-evident to anyone who spends more than a month in Italy. The real point is that when the executive body is so deeply entrenched, protected moreover by ancient codices that date back to Justinian, reform from the top is a slow and heart-breaking process that must inevitably take decades.

With a divided, partisan Press, the most well-meaning movements can be quickly discredited for party purposes. When Gronchi left for America for his vital discussions with Eisenhower, the Italian Press was full of juicy pictures and juicy copy about the Montesi scandal. Most of the Press gave Gronchi and Eisenhower a contemptuous half column.

Again the question: where do you start, with any hope of foreseeable success?

I have one answer. I believe it to be the true one. Before I give it to you, let me explain something else. There are two Italies—the North and the South. The North begins at Rome and ends on the borders of France, Switzerland and Austria. The South begins at Terracina and ends where the heel of Calabria and the toe of Sicily dip into the sea.

They are two different countries. The people look different, they dress differently, they talk differently, they think differently. They have a different past and, I believe, a different future. What I have studied and written applies to the South; it has not necessarily the same application in the North. The South is deeply entrenched in the feudal tradition of lords and servants, of conquerors and conquered.

What shocks the visitor, therefore, is accepted as a commonplace by the gentry of the South. There have always been poor in Naples. There have always been scugnizzi. The peasants have always been sharecroppers. The functionaries have always been underpaid. When you tell them that these are anachronisms, dangerous, even explosive in the twentieth century, they shrug and turn away.

When a poor man becomes rich in Naples—and some of them did become rich during the war—he becomes a beggar on horseback, aping the vices of the *signori*, contemptuous of the misery from which he sprang.

If you want an illustration of the difference between this country and Australia or America or even England, you have it here. In these countries it has become the ornament

of riches to turn them to charitable purposes, to found
schools and endow universities. The triumph of the hos-
tess is to give a bigger charity ball than her rival. Here,
when you make money, you invest most of it in America,
build yourself a villa on Capri, and pay your servants a
dollar a day!

Rome is 150 miles from Naples, but for political and
social purposes it might well be 15,000. The reform of the
South, therefore, must begin in the South.

I believe, very strongly, that it must begin with the
Church of the South.

This is a strong statement, but I make it with measured
conviction. Italian anti-clericals will smile when they read
it. Catholics abroad may well look askance at its bluntness.
If I were not a Catholic myself they might well accuse me
of sectarian bias. But, because I am a Catholic, I understand
my own Church. I know its strength and I know its human
weaknesses. I understand how deeply it enters into the
lives of this people, even into the lives of those who have
turned away from it. I know that if it were taken away,
with its pageantry and its pomp and its solid core of belief
in the dignity of individual man, this people would sink
into a far greater misery. I speak, therefore, with the frank-
ness of one of the family.

The Church of the South shares the feudal origins of the
people. Much of its possession in lands, in buildings, in
accumulated treasures of gold and silver reliquaries, in
jewelled statues and the rest, came from the succession of
feudal rulers. In this respect it differs not at all from the
Church in France, in England and Southern Germany.

Where it does differ is in the taint of nepotism that still
clings to it. Nepotism is unavoidable where you have an
established religion and the bulk of the population are believers. If you're all Catholics, it's unavoidable that some-

body's uncle must be a bishop and somebody else's cousin a cardinal or an abbot. It is equally natural that family influence is going to be exercised to secure advantage or preferment either in the Church or through it.

When the Bishop's nephew happens to be a banker who pays insurance money to the Communist Party, or an employer who pays sweatshop wages and refuses the right of the worker to organise, the guilt of the one tends to stain the presumptive virtue of the other.

When the Mayor of Naples builds a new square instead of a school and the Cardinal of Naples doesn't preach a sermon about the anomaly, even the most long-suffering faithful want to know why. When a local *cavaliere*, who is known to have worked a loan from the Cassa del Mezzogiorno and diverted it to his enterprise in the North, appears at the Easter ceremonies wearing a Papal decoration or is received as a guest of the Cardinal, the scandal is inevitable.

When the brown Capuccini or the little Black Sisters beg in the streets of Naples, the people accept it without question. They know that there are half a dozen works of charity being supported by these mendicant funds—orphanages, foundling homes, a refuge for old people. But they ask why it is always the poor who give, and why they don't hear the sermon of the rich man and Lazarus preached from the Sunday pulpit.

It is preached, but not often enough and not in every church. The most frequent criticism I heard about the Church of the Mezzogiorno was: 'it accommodates itself to the situation'. The Italian phrase is expressive. It connotes acceptance, tolerance. It hints at participation.

I, myself, have sat, Sunday after Sunday, at early and late Masses and have not heard one word of social justice or criticism of social evils. I have heard pious clichés and well-worn annotations, but passionate condemnation of known and widespread evils, no! There is no Fulton Sheen in·the South of Italy, though God knows there is need of men like him.

The work of men like Borrelli is the more remarkable for the difficult climate in which it is performed.

There are good men, earnest men, enlightened men, but too often they are not heard because of the vacillation or conservatism of the hierarchy.

If all this sounds too general and one-sided, think for a moment of this point. Naples is a city of two million people. All but a minute fraction belong, at least in name, to the Church. They are baptised Catholics. A Catholic may reject his faith, but he never quite loses the mark of it. Few, even of those who do not practise their faith, will commit themselves to open disrespect for the clergy or open rebellion against a clear precept. Certainly not here in the Mezzogiorno. The most cynical politician makes certain of showing up in Church round election time. The least devout mayor will not risk an open breach with the Bishop.

Therefore the Church has power. It has spiritual power over the devout and practising. It has the power of public opinion to wield against those who profess but do not practise. If it does not use this power, it is because too many of its clergy have accommodated themselves to the situation and too few have the courage or enlightenment to challenge it.

*　　*　　*

If you would like it brought a little closer to home, let me tell you the tale of Greta's housemaid.

Greta is a good friend of ours. She is a Swede, married to an Italian, who is the nephew of a bishop. She is a Catholic, so she, too, is part of the family.

138

Greta's maid was a mountain girl, engaged to a lad from the coast. Her *fidanzato* became impatient in the warm spring weather, and the maid became scared that she might lose him.

So, two months later Greta was faced with a problem, a maid who was a maid no longer, a weeping girl who was afraid to go home because her father would beat her and call her harsh names and turn her out of the house. What was she to do? Her fidanzato wasn't sure he wanted to marry a ruined girl. She had no money to pay what the midwife would ask for an abortion. She lacked the courage to throw herself over the cliff.

Greta, being a wise and gentle woman, pointed out that none of these things was really necessary. She, herself, would explain matters to the family. If they didn't want the girl at home, well, she had a room in Greta's house. If the fidanzato didn't want to marry her, then she should have the baby. Greta and her husband would pay the expenses. The child would be welcomed and cared for. After a while the girl was calmed and Greta set off on stage one of the peace-making operations.

The family was adamant. The father, a peasant farmer, shut his door and his heart against the erring daughter. The girl had made herself a *puttana*! Let her go and join the others on the streets of Naples.

Whereat, Greta got angry—and her anger is something to see. It has a rich and bawdy quality which awed the simple family and bent their stubbornness to a modest compromise. They would not disown the daughter. If she persuaded the fidanzato to marry her, the mother would come to the wedding, but none of the others. They would not receive her back into the house. That was too much!

Stage two was the fidanzato. He was a stolid, loutish fellow who hummed and ha'd and mumbled in dialect and refused to give a definite answer. He might marry the girl. He might not. He would have to see. His family might not like the idea of his marrying a pregnant woman. On him, too, Greta turned her anger, and, though he still made no promises, she sensed that he was frightened of what the *signora* might be able to do to him.

So far, so good. The sky was beginning to clear, when lo! a new cloud on the horizon. The *parroco*—the parish priest! The parroco was an elderly man with grey hair and a kindly face. He had come, he said, to counsel the signora.

Greta folded her hands in her lap and smiled sweetly and waited for the counsel. It was blunt and simple. The presence of a ruined girl in the signora's house was a scandal in the town, a scandal that would become more apparent as the months drew on. He would counsel the signora to get rid of the girl as soon as possible.

Greta smiled blandly and asked if the parroco had any suggestions. He was a little vague about it. He thought that there was a house for such unfortunates in Naples. Greta mentioned with some acerbity the possibility that she might never reach Naples. The girl was distraught, lost and unhappy. She might very well throw herself over a cliff.

The parroco shrugged. The girl was ruined anyway. What was more important was to preserve the innocence of the rest of the population. Greta, who had little faith in the innocence and a wide acquaintance with the primitive morals of the township, was unimpressed. She gave the parroco the rough edge of her tongue. He went away a very unhappy man.

Came next the Mother Superior of the local convent for a woman-to-woman talk on the same theme: scandal in the village. Greta suggested she might care to give the girl a home in the convent and hide the scandal in the most effective way of all. The Mother Superior hid her face in horror at the thought.

Finally Greta's husband was called for a cup of coffee and a quiet chat with his uncle, the Bishop. The exact substance of the talk was not revealed to me, but ever since relations between uncle and nephew have been somewhat strained.

Later, before the scandal got too great, the housemaid married her fidanzato and the storm in the tea cup abated.

The point of the story is not the comedy, but the fact that this primitive puritanism is still widespread among the clergy of the South.

It is not Christianity. It is not Catholicism. It is not to be accepted as a display of village ignorance. The ignorance exists, surely, but the parroco is appointed to dispel it and teach charity and kindness. In this case, as in so many others, he had accommodated himself to the situation, and the Bishop was prepared to back him.

Quis custodiet ipsos custodes? I wouldn't know, but they certainly need looking after here in the South.

* * *

The root of it again is education. You can't expect a fledgling priest, raw and uncertain of himself, to fight the evil unless he has been trained to see it, and unless he knows that his bishop will back him to the last frightening consequence of the Gospel truth. You can't expect the bishop to back him, if the bishop has, by weakness or indiscretion, accepted a gift for his Church or his charities from a source which is known to be tainted.

The charities of Naples need funds desperately. The House of the Urchins is only one case in point. But funds should be rejected—and publicly rejected—if they are known to be the price of silence or 'accommodation' at election time.

If family relationships are involved, then they must not be allowed to influence the preaching of the truth.

Look at it another way. Think how many churches there are in Naples. I can't tell you the number. I doubt if there are many who can. But in Sorrento, a town of ten to twelve thousand inhabitants, there are twenty-eight! If, in every church of Naples and the Peninsula, there were preached, on the same day, a vital, compelling sermon on the evils of the South, their causes and their remedies, with names, dates and places, how many people would it reach and what would be its effect? The Cardinal of Naples has the power to order it to be done. He has facts and figures and names enough to make a hundred sermons. He has priests to preach them twenty times over. Why isn't it done?

Sometimes it is a question of political expediency: the Italian Church is backing the Christian Democrats, who, like any other party, have their share of promoters and place-hunters. Sometimes it is administrative caution inside the bureaucracy of the Church. Sometimes it is fear that certain sources of charitable funds may dry up if personalities are aired from the pulpit.

I state it now, bluntly and without equivocation, that some of the clergy of the South have used the confessional to win votes—especially the women's votes—for the Christian Democratic Party. To claim that is part of the fight against Communism is an evil folly. To claim that the end justifies or even condones the means, is a denial of Christian faith.

Confession is a sacrament of the Catholic Church, a private tribunal secret to God and the individual soul, a place of shriving, a channel of grace.

To pervert it to a political weapon is to destroy it, and the faith of the people as well.

It is all wrong, dangerously wrong. The Church was founded on twelve poor fishermen and the gospel truth. I have yet to hear it pronounced from the chair of Peter that party funds and accommodation to a situation, even Vatican diplomacy, will do more for the world than truth, justice and the grace of God.

There is another side to the argument, of course.

You can't lay all the sins of its members at the door of the Church. The Church's function is to preach the truth and open the channels of grace. The individual is still free to accept or reject them. That is true. The Church's function is spiritual; it can be negated by the free will of the member.

But here, in Italy, the Church is already committed to the temporal order. It is committed historically by the nature of its growth, economically by its possessions, politically by its open championship of a given political party. Therefore it lays itself open to free criticism on fields of activity.

If its political actions and associations are not free of taint, then they must be made so. If its economic situation involves it with people who want to use its influence for their own ends, then it must disengage itself at whatever cost. If no such involvement exists, then this fact should be preached—and clearly—because there are many honest people who believe that it does exist.

The winter of 1956 was a brutal one for the peasant farmers of Italy. American Catholic organisations donated thousands of bushels of grain-seed for free distribution in the most distressed areas.

This grain was distributed under the direction of executives and officials of the Confederazione dei Coltivatori

Diretti, a political organisation said to represent the rural interests. On the voting figures only forty-six per cent of the farmers are members of the Confederazione.

There were complaints that the grain had been distributed only to registered members of the Party who then had to pay a part of its value in cold cash.

I cannot say whether the accusation is true or not. Certainly I heard no denials of it. The important thing, for the purposes of this argument, is the involvement of the Church. The gift was made by American Catholics to a distressed peasantry who were all co-religionists. If the accusation was true, it is the duty of the Church authorities to expose the scandal. If it was not true, the Church should dissociate itself from the accusation. In neither case can it remain silent. So far as I have been able to discover, it has not said a word.

The Church, Holy, Roman Catholic and Apostolic, demands from all its members obedience to a rigorous moral law. It must apply the same law to the administration of its Southern Italian Province.

* * *

Now, there's another story to tell, about the author.

The story begins with our hiring our first maid, by name, Angela. We hired her with the aid of an American friend of twenty years standing in Italy. We were assured that she came of a good, peasant family, that she was strong, healthy, willing, intelligent and, above all, honest. She had been educated to third grade and she spoke Italian and dialect. I don't speak dialect, so the Italian was a necessary accomplishment.

We hired her. We thought that, as she was a local and honest, she would probably save us money at the market. We thought that, if she were going to cook, she'd better do her own marketing. The Sorrentines have a way of hoisting the price the moment a stranger gets within bargaining distance. So we gave her 5000 lire and sent her off to do the shopping.

There was no change from the 5000, but in our innocence we thought that was fair enough. We were starting housekeeping. There were cupboards to be stocked, staple condiments to be bought, and besides it's bad policy for the master or the mistress to be too interfering in the kitchen, especially in the first week.

So we gave Angela her head, for one week, during which time she went through 25,000 lire without a blink. I wouldn't have minded the expense if I could have seen the results of it at the table. But I didn't. The meat was poor, the cooking was worse, even the wine was sour and watered. When we went thunderously, to make our accounting in the kitchen, the cupboards were stacked with tins and tins of food, which we'd never eat in a hundred years—even if we liked it, which we didn't!

There were jars of anchovies and tins of artichokes, pickled peppers and bottles of olives. There were tins of sockeye salmon and jars of English jam; but no flour, no sugar, no pepper, no salt.

We looked at one another. We laughed our heads off. Why not? We had paid 25,000 lire for the privilege! Angela was honest all right. All the items tallied. But she had no more idea of shopping or spending money economically and advantageously than she had of flying to the moon. Every day she had gone down to Sorrento with her purse full of money and her little heart full of pride. She was the *cameriera* of the *gran' scrittore australiano*. If anybody doubted it, just let them watch her splurge to prove it!

The moral of my little tale? *Caveat* America!

America is involved as much as the Church and the industrialists and the old families in this question of social reform. She is involved, because she is pouring money into the country. She has a duty and a right to ask where this money goes. So has the taxpayer, who believes that the funds mulcted from him each year are being used to build a strong economy and a bulwark against Communism.

That's the principle. The effect in the South is entirely the opposite. The constant unemployment, the hunger and the hopelessness, the atmosphere of mistrust and corruption, the frightening inertia in the face of more frightening misery, all these things are sharp weapons in the hands of the Communist Party. They are weapons forged in America with taxpayers' money.

What's to do about it? Here are a few suggestions.

Under the United Nations Charter America has no right to interfere in the affairs of a partner nation. But when she is the banker for that nation, she has a banker's right to ask for an accounting. I say again the accounting she gets in Rome is not a true one. Why? Because as I have shown, figures about Italy are misleading. The facts have to be seen to be understood.

A rural bank manager takes an occasional trip out to his client's farm to see how he runs it. Why not send a few experts down to the South, officially or unofficially, to measure the progress of land reform and the needs of peasant communities? Let them ask why whole villages have been cleaned out by emigration while productive areas lie useless. Let them see how much money has been wasted on election-time projects that have never been brought to completion. Let them ask, as Dayton did, why bank money costs so much when cheap money is needed for agricultural and industrial development.

Education is the beginning of progress and reform.

Have a few educators come down here to the South and report on what they find. Let some of the research foundations send out economists and sociologists to look in on the skin game. And make sure that their reports are publicised and tabled in Congress before the next loans are approved!

And keep the investigators out of the deceptively congenial atmosphere of Rome and Florence and Venice! The Italians can better the British in the gentle art of 'duchessing'. Rome is a city of diplomats and contact men. It is far, far away from the harsh realities of the Mezzogiorno. But the truth is down here, the real truth about this seductive and devious country. And America and its citizens, like all the rest of the Western world, have great need to know it.

To put it more bluntly, there is in the Italian character, especially in the Southern character, a wide streak of irresponsibility and a vanity that makes them unwilling to admit it.

A young blood of Naples will scrimp and save and put himself in hock to buy a Vespa or a Fiat runabout. Then he will tear the tripes out of the engine and strip the brakes down to the shoe metal and rip tyres down to the thread by driving it like a maniac.

If he's doing it on his own money, it's his own business. But if he's doing it on yours or mine, it's better to teach him sense before he wrecks the outfit.

* * *

All this, of course, is only the beginning. It rests with the Church to prepare a state of mind receptive to the principles of social justice. It rests with America to demand responsible control in the allocation and use of dollar funds. But unless the money-holders of Italy—landowners, industrialists, investors—undertake their own house-cleaning, there will be no reform. Unless they realise that their only hope of a permanent, peaceful economy lies in a healthy balanced industrial system, they will not set themselves to achieve it.

These men are afraid of what they are doing now. Why else do they try to move their funds out to America? Why do they try to prevent the organisation of the workers? Why have they formed the Fronte Padronale—the association of industrialists, landowners and merchants, which is pledged to arrest all movement for better wages and working conditions? Why have they split the unions into two groups—top management and lower employees? Why do they nurse the one and keep the other down to breadline subsistence? Because they are afraid.

Here in the South they build high walls about their villas and fit them with electric gates and keep a wolf-hound chained in the garden, to keep out the beggars and the poor.

You and I live in reasonable comfort with an open garden and a gate that any tradesman can vault over. We are not afraid, because by evolution and common effort and the spread of social principles we have achieved a reasonably balanced, democratic society.

In the Mezzogiorno there are few who are willing to work for democratic progress, because there are many who don't believe in it. They know how to achieve it, but they refuse the means at their disposal. More than this, they fight actively against it.

They are intelligent men, yet they want to put the clock back. They may well succeed. The Fronte Padronale is the best way to get the Fronte Popolare back to Italy. The Communists don't have to work in Italy. They can sit back and let the signori work for them. Using American dollars!

CHAPTER NINE

ONE FINE spring day I drove into Naples to visit a big industrial concern. I went at the personal invitation of the family which owns it. They had heard I was writing this book. They were aware of my strictures on the skin game of Italy. They did not challenge my findings. They did ask, however, that, in fairness to themselves and to others like them, I visit the Naples factory and see what had been done towards the application of modern social principles and what might be done by others with good will and good economic sense.

The Cirio Company is one of the largest canning enterprises in Europe. Its products are exported all over the world. It has a big plant in Argentina. It operates factories in the South and in the North. It has farms at Salerno and Mondragone and elsewhere. Its headquarters are in Naples.

One of the most interesting things about it for the purposes of this book is that the majority of the shares are all held by one family—the Signorini. All the decisions therefore have the seal of what is virtually a family council. In a country like this with a pool of two to three million unemployed, the company could function as a tight little autarchy without regard to social principles. Instead, its worker relationships, like its production-line techniques, bear comparison with the most evolved organisation in America, Great Britain and Australia.

The Naples factory sprawls over a dozen blocks on both sides of the road in the notorious San Giovanni district. It is within a stone's throw of the worst hovels on the Via Marittima. It is right in the centre of some of the poorest and oldest tenement houses in the city. Few areas of Naples can compare with this for poverty, unemployment and abject misery. The observer has, therefore, the benefit of natural contrast.

Both factory areas are enclosed by high stone walls and the entrances are barred by heavily reinforced gates which are opened only to permit the passage of necessary traffic.

My guide was the American wife of the senior brother of the family. As we drove in through the main gate, a guard saluted smartly and motioned us to a parking space in a wide asphalt courtyard. Another guard rushed to open the door and we were conducted with ceremony to the door of the administrative building. We were introduced to two of the brothers Signorini and to the son of our American friend.

We were shown a ground plan of the organisation—its farms, its production centres, its distributing organisation. It was impressive and it looked efficient. A tour of the factory area confirmed the impression. The machinery was modern, the production methods were as good and in some cases better than those I had seen in other parts of the world. The workers wore clean uniforms and they seemed to work happily. All of which meant very little to my investigation. A food processing plant has to be clean. It has to be efficient if it wants to make money in a competitive market. Most production-line workers look intent on their jobs. In Naples they have to look that way because there are 200,000 waiting to take their place.

What interested me most of all was what the company was doing for its staff.

There are some 1500 permanent workers in the San Giovanni factory. This number is more than doubled in the picking season. Necessarily the majority of the workers on the processing lines are women. This again is common to food plants throughout the world. Many of the women are married because the company makes it a policy to give employment to married women in a city of so many workless men.

You take it for granted in Naples that all married women have children. The children of the Cirio workers are the first thought of the company.

After our inspection of the plant, we were taken in hand by the personnel manager, who drove us out of the plant into a small side street. Here the Signorini brothers had founded an elementary school for the children of their workers. Before I went in, I had prepared myself for yet another repetition of the dusty, shop-worn look of Italian schools. I didn't get it. I found myself in a modern building with bright airy classrooms, freshly-painted walls, spotless floors and modern teaching equipment. The children's faces shone with cleanliness and health. All were dressed in freshly laundered smocks with white collars and bows of different coloured ribbons to indicate their classes. The teachers were bright-eyed young women, each with an Elementary Teacher's Diploma. The Directress was a senior officer of the Education Department. I looked carefully at the exercise books and the class projects. They were in immaculate order and of a uniformly high standard.

The classrooms were ranged around a large central room, the school dining room. Here, each day, the children were given a hot midday meal in accordance with a dietary chart prepared by the food chemists of the company. At the mid-morning recess each child was given a glass of fresh pasteurised milk.

The kindergarten room contained a small but elaborate stage and from the window of this room I could see a wide open playground with monkey-bars and roundabouts of tubular steel. By any standard, the school for the Cirio children was first-class.

The children are taken into the kindergarten at the age of three and are given the full elementary course of five grades. All the expenses of the school—textbooks, uniforms, daily meals, regular medical attention, the salaries of the teachers and the stipend of a permanent chaplain—are paid by the company. Only the Directress is a salaried employee of the Comune.

When I looked at the bright rooms and the bright faces, when I recalled that many of these children lived in the overcrowded tenements of San Giovanni, I could not help comparing them with the other children I had seen—the scrabbling mites on the rubbish heaps, the babes eaten by flies in the baracche, the child-workers in the back streets off the Via Roma.

I thought of the 50,000 others who had no schools at all. I wondered why the other big companies of Naples hadn't taken up the idea. It seemed to me a much more profitable investment than the hush-money paid to Communist funds to call off a railway strike.

I remembered, too, the problem of Don Borrelli: what to do with his boys after they had finished their sketchy elementary education. I put this one to the personnel manager.

"We are one company," he said. "What we do must be for our own people first. It is our idea that when these children are educated, we send the bright ones to technical school and later absorb them into our own employment. We cannot do more. Already this project is a heavy charge on the company's revenue. We need not do it. With so many unemployed, we could fill our staff ten times over, but the Signorini family have a social conscience. They are good Italians. They are good Neapolitans."

After what I had seen, I was prepared to believe that. But there was more to come.

The personnel manager piled us in the car again and drove us back to the main factory. We went up a flight of stairs and found ourselves in a large and airy room which looked like the nursery of a large maternity hospital. The walls were pastel-tinted; the new venetian blinds made a pleasing colour contrast. There were about thirty cribs in the room, each furnished with fresh linen and bright baby blankets, each with its own active little occupant. They squalled or slept or chewed their fists as healthily as any children in the more fortunate countries of the world.

There were three maternity sisters in attendance, each fully trained in obstetrics and infant welfare. There was a row of spotless porcelain baths and a shining modern kitchenette with a steriliser and cooking equipment.

When a factory mother returned to work after her confinement, the babes were taken in charge by the nursery and the mothers came at fixed times to breast-feed them.

The nursing mothers go straight to a feeding room where they wash and change into clean white smocks provided by the company. The children are brought to them from the nursery and a nurse superintends the feeding, in case supplementary diet is required. At no time are the mothers allowed to enter the nursery itself.

Apart from its value to mother and child, this system provides the best piece of education in cleanliness and baby welfare that I have yet seen in Naples. Both mothers and babies return at night to the crowded tenements of the bassi, and their good fortune is the envy of those who have neither work nor education nor opportunity to offer to their children.

Across the street from the factory is a club provided by the company for Cirio workers, with radio, television and reading material. Further away is a large sports arena and the living and training quarters of the professional soccer team maintained by the company.

All in all it adds up to a solid social achievement comparable to what Olivetti has done in his own field. But it does not end here. The company maintains its own farms for the improvement of orchard and dairy products. Workers on these farms are provided with model houses fully furnished at a rental scaled to their earning capacity in the company. There are pension schemes and generous cover for incapacity arising out of sickness or accident.

In the red belt of San Giovanni, the work of this company is a shining example of what free enterprise can do to lift the living standards of the depressed South. It is also a bleak reproach to the many others who might do the same but so far have done nothing.

My final note is made with no hint of malice. The gates of this workers' paradise are guarded by men with loaded pistols: an unavoidable necessity since the store rooms and the freezing chambers of the Cirio Company are stacked with food products, while half a mile away are the grim hovels where people sleep fifteen in a room and women sell themselves to buy food for their children.

* * *

By the time I came to set my notes in order for this chapter, I was tired and irritable. I wanted to make a constructive book, to point to the good things as well as the bad. To show where reforms had begun in the South and the help they needed to stimulate their growth. Too many writers—too many Italian writers—had made profitable theatre out of the miseries of Naples. I wanted to do something more.

The Cirio factory was one hopeful sign. Borrelli, himself, was a dramatic exemplar of reform. I was looking for others like them, but outside the clergy and in other fields of service and social development.

I had been bitterly disappointed. I had begun many lines of inquiry, but all of them had led me inevitably to the Neapolitan skin markets.

Housing, for instance. I had come back to Naples after five years' absence. The first thing that impressed me was the growth of new apartment blocks southward from Naples, along the coastal strip and right through to Torre del Greco and Castellamare. Some of them were being erected as private projects, others as part of a Government housing scheme financed by the Cassa del Mezzogiorno.

I had just finished building a house in my own country, so my head was stuffed full of facts and figures and I had a painful and personal acquaintance with the problems of the investor and the builder. I began by tramping through the unfinished shells, watching the working methods, studying the layout.

The first thing that impressed me was wasteful design. The architects had thrown away hundreds of square feet of living space in every block. In a block of ten apartments, there was living space for fifteen, but most of it was wasted on wide foyers and triple-width staircases—living space that had no built-in cupboards, so that it would be halved when the heavy Neapolitan furniture was moved in. The architects of the South seemed never to have opened an overseas manual on low-cost housing. Their laundry facilities were limited to the primitive cement washtub without hot water and there was no communal drying space for clothes. So, naturally, they were still hung on the balconies, as they were in the bassi.

This, for all its seriousness, was only wasteful planning. When I looked at the cost sheets, I was staggered. With a labour cost one tenth of that prevailing in Australia, the cost of building was twenty-five per cent higher! Why? Materials, they told me: cement and stone and ceramic tiles. But these same materials were produced with the same cheap labour? Certainly, but the suppliers put on big profit margins. To justify some of the prices I saw, the profit margin must have been nearly 500 per cent. Of course, with a bankrate up to seventeen per cent, everything else goes haywire.

But there was more yet. There is a shortage of skilled artisans and a famine dearth of cost accountants and quantity surveyors. So the job supervisor is able to make a handsome rakeoff from the agencies handling business materials. Bills are falsified and the difference split both ways. One builder to whom I spoke had just succeeded, after twelve months' investigation, in tracing 500,000 lire *a month* lost in gerrymandered costs!

Because there is no effective control, and because most of the South is held in feudal right by old families, land costs are hoisted out of all proportion to real value.

So the skin game goes on—unreal land values, loaded building costs, wasteful construction—and no hope at all for ownership or reasonable rental.

I asked about child welfare and mothercraft centres. They told me there were some in Naples. I believed that. But in all the days and nights of tramping the streets swarming with ragged children, I didn't see any. I did see a rash of doctors' placards—*Doctor X, Specialista, Veneree e Malattia di Pelle!*

District nursing? House visitation by social workers? Group welfare? The Sisters of Charity did some of that, they told me. They went into the houses of the distressed poor, they scrubbed floors and washed the sick and prepared meals and changed the babies. But social work apart from the Church, paid or unpaid? Very little. Welfare work, in spite of the existence of a Department of Public Welfare, was practically non-existent. Why? A shrug and a significant gesture—the Church controls all that!

You will probably have gathered long before this that I hold no brief for the defence of the Church in the South. I am able to view with a certain sympathy the anti-clericalism of Italy. I am able to understand the historic and social reasons for it. But the fact remains that no Italian, however anti-clerical, has been able to point to any comparable work done by secular organisations.

When I challenged them with this argument, they would launch into long explanations of the secular intrusion of the Church, its political accommodation, the compromises of the hierarchy. But not one of them ever gave me a satisfactory answer as to why none of the critics had ever rolled up his sleeves and done what Borrelli had done, or Don Gnocchi in the North. They admitted that these men were not part of the hierarchy or the bureaucracy of the Church. They admitted that what they had done was achieved with courage and personal effort. Why couldn't the critics do the same? The answer was always a deprecating shrug. I was a foreigner. I could not be expected to understand.

I was prepared to understand. I wanted facts, and I was prepared to accept them from the Devil himself, but I wanted to be shown chapter and verse. Nobody has yet offered me a page-reference.

You should understand that I was looking for the answer to a specific problem: how best to create for the boys in the House of the Urchins an opportunity, a hopeful future. Ideally, the future should be in their own country, even if it were created by initial help from well-wishers overseas.

A work of this kind has a double value. It benefits those for whom it is created. It ennobles those who take part in it and it spreads, as ripples spread in a pond, touching many others, setting off new currents of movement and action. Transfer the work to another country and you yield to the counsel of despair. You say, "There is no hope here. Let us start somewhere else!"

I have stopped half way to this conclusion. There is hope for Italy and specifically for the South. The existence of a work like Borrelli's affirms that. But it will be decades before the hope is realised and in any year of those decades the hope can be wrecked.

For the boys, themselves, there is no hope. Borrelli has taken them as far as he can in the conditions that exist to-day. Their only chance is to get out and begin a new life overseas.

*　　*　　*

Let me tell you two simple stories. The first contains the germ of future hope. The second illustrates the despair of the present.

One fine April day, after a gruelling week in Naples, I took time off from my notebooks and went down to visit the Marina Grande, the small circular cove at the north end of the town of Sorrento.

My guide was Giuliana Benzoni, a crackling, vital woman, a violent opponent of the old régime, whose record as an underground courier during the war makes a hair-raising story. She walked me down a flight of worn stairs under a Greek archway and down to the small cobbled beach, where the fisherfolk live and the boat-builders who make the skiffs for all the villages from Massa to Capri.

The folk of the Marina Grande are not Italians at all. They are descendants of the Barbary Corsairs, who pillaged this coast in the old days. Their dialect is tinged with Arabic and, until the last two decades, they lived completely apart from the townfolk of the peninsula, who called them *i barbari*—the barbarians.

They did not marry outside their own beachhead and centuries of in-breeding have produced some quaint biological phenomena. Now, however, there is new blood among them—Italian, German, British, American. You see tow-heads and apple-cheeks sprouting among the dark, narrow-faced Berber families.

They are a gentle, primitive folk with weathered faces and ready smiles for the visitor who cares to spend a little patience and politeness on them. They are slow-moving and slow of speech like all fishermen, and for all their bare feet and their patched clothes and the sparse simplicity of their lives they have a great natural dignity.

You see them rarely in the town. The commerce of their lives is carried on between the house fronts and the sea, among the beached boats and the trailing nets and along the great stone ramp that leads up to the hilltop.

In winter their life is hard and frugal; but, when the summer comes and the fish are back with the warm currents and the tourists come to hire their boats, they do better. At night you see their clustered lights over the fishing grounds and in the morning you see the women squatting on the beach or on the sea-wall, patching the fine, brown nets.

Their houses are old and crumbling, piled one on top of another like children's blocks, and in the dim rooms on the ground level the meticulous craftsmen build the long double-ended boats to the pattern of their Moorish ancestors.

Their children are brown-faced, bare-footed and shy as young horses; but they have bright eyes and wide, winning smiles. In the morning they go to school in the Sisters' convent, and in the afternoon they do the housework or the shopping or romp noisily among the boats drawn up on the stony beach.

We picked out way over the pebbles, greeting this one and that, hailing a child or two, and enquiring after the health of an aged grandmother huddled under her shawls in the late, cool sunlight. Finally, we climbed a flight of stone steps to a first-floor room in one of the water-front houses.

To my surprise, it was full of children—thirty-six I counted, but they told me some were absent. Although it was late in the afternoon, long past school time, they were all busy over their books. Some were working out problems in elementary arithmetic, some were reading geography books, others were drawing or making paper cutouts.

There was no teacher; but three girls and two young men, seventeen to twenty years of age, moved among them helping them with their work. They were well dressed. Their faces were handsome and intelligent. Their approach to the children was affectionate and interested.

After we had watched a while they called the youngsters to the centre of the floor and led them through a series of songs and folk dances.

There was something strangely touching about the drab, dusty room with the ragged infants and their spruce young instructors. The kids were so obviously interested, their monitors were so patently proud of the work they were doing. As they bustled back to their desks, Giuliana Benzoni explained to me.

The young instructors were students, one of engineering, another of architecture, a third of economics. They belonged to a club which met every evening after lectures and whose members took it in turns to come down to the Marina Grande and give after-school lessons to the fisher children. They took no pay and asked no thanks, and each year they paid their own expenses to the Summer School of the Assistenti Sociali in Rome, to learn more about the education of under-privileged children.

I looked at them with new interest. This was the sort of thing I had been looking for in the South, and of which I had found so little—the spontaneous, unselfish movement of youth towards social reform, outside the party framework of political sponsorship. The girls were young, attractive and vital. Most Neapolitan girls who can afford it spend the years between puberty and marriage in sacred meditation on boys, bed, clothes, local gossip. They tend to develop the vacant comfortable look of pneumatic cushions. Not so these. They had intelligent eyes and intelligent conversation. They wanted to go places, they needed only someone to show them the way.

They had found that someone in Giuliana Benzoni. She had founded the club and introduced its members to the idea of social service. She supplied them with books and kept them in contact with visiting celebrities.

The following afternoon I sat with them in the big basement room of her villa, watching Ruth Draper giving one of her memorable performances.

The youngsters had taken eagerly to the idea of unselfish service and the need in Italy for a beginning, however small. They were hungry for knowledge and for contact with the outside world. When I talked to them in their club room, their eyes shone with interest and their questions on economics, politics and social organisations went straight to the core of the matter.

When I enquired into their backgrounds, I found that they all came from small middle-class families—the 90,000 lire a month bracket of teachers, bank clerks and accountants. None of them belonged to the signorial families or to the new class of post-war merchants. This, too, was significant. Democracy, as we know it, is founded on a strong, prosperous middle-class. Here in Italy, the middle-class is ill-paid, insecure and caught between the upper and nether millstones of irresponsible capital and unemployed labour.

What these boys and girls were doing was all the more important and all the more unselfish. It stood as a stinging reproach to the critics and the politicos who talked so much and did damn-all.

* * *

The next one is a golf story. It has nothing to do with my handicap or how my professional told me to handle the dog-leg on the fifteenth. So you may read it with comparative safety.

High up on the spine of the Sorrentine mountains, just past Saint Agatha of the Two Gulfs, is a long stretch of undulating land. It belongs to the Comune of Sorrento, and is, in fact, one of the few tracts of common land available in these parts. You reach it by a scenic motor road and when you get there the view is breath-taking. There is the Bay of Naples on one side and the Gulf of Salerno on the other. There is a majesty of cliffs and blue water, and a nestling of red-tiled towns, and a march of orchard trees through the valleys and up the steep hillsides.

A Sorrentine friend, a nominee for the new committee of the Comune, drove me up to see it. After I'd admired the view, I mentioned casually that it would make a wonderful golf course. My friend chuckled happily—the Comune had the same idea. When we went back to town, he would show me the plans. They had been drawn by a well-known British expert. They included a nine-hole course, a small hotel and a chair lift up from the town of Sorrento.

The project interested me. It had imagination and good

prospects. It would attract a new type of tourist. It would develop the winter trade. It could make Sorrento a permanent sojourn spot, instead of a jumping-off place for Capri and Ischia. It would give the foreign visitors more to do than sit in the Piazza or wander round the shops in boredom and frustration. Its construction and maintenance would provide more employment for the locals. All in all, it was a sound progressive proposition.

I was anxious to hear more of it.

We drove back to town to look over the plans. The course looked interesting. The British expert had done a good job. The hotel layout was modern and comfortable. The chairlift would be a separate investment by the Circumvesuviana Railway. That left only the course and the hotel to be financed by the Comune.

Ah, no! My friend smiled gently at my simplicity. Not by the Comune.

By private enterprise then? A lease of the land to an Italian company?

No, again! The Comune was trying, without much hope of success, to raise some capital in London from English investors!

I was dumbfounded. I said so, bluntly. There was enough idle capital on the peninsula to finance the project ten times over. The land itself, at present inflated values, was security enough for a substantial bank loan. There were thousands of unemployed on the peninsula. In the winter months there would be even more. Why go abroad for capital? Why not make it an Italian enterprise?

My friend shrugged unhappily. The conversation had taken an unexpected turn. He pointed out, with obvious reluctance, that risk capital cost a lot less in England and that, in any case, Italian investors were a chary lot and difficult to handle. Italian banks were the most difficult of all.

Besides, it was such a sound prospect, why shouldn't the British be interested?

Politeness forbade the obvious answer. Investment depends on *fiducia*—confidence. If the Italians had so little confidence in their own country, in the good sense of its financiers, in the honesty of its commercial and administrative system, how could they expect the British to have more?

*　　*　　*

I repeated this story the same afternoon to Professor Gaetano Salvemini, formerly of Harvard University and now living in retirement at Capo di Sorrento. Salvemini is an old man now, but he is one of the world's great humanists and he is one of the incorruptibles in this corrupt and despairing country.

He is over eighty years old, yet his eyes sparkle and his face shines with the eternal youth of the Mediterranean sun. His retreat at the wooded bluff above Sorrento is a meeting place for hope-hungry Italian students, and a goal of pilgrimage for those who studied under him in the New World.

His verdict on my story was delivered in the calm, measured voice which still bears traces of its Calabrian peasant accent.

"In this, my friend, you see the fate of a nation which loses faith in itself because it has lost faith in the truth. When men do not believe in liberty, they put themselves in the power of others to find an illusion of security. They are unwilling to take risks, because they are afraid of sacrifice. They have lost their dignity as men, so they are content to make themselves beggars. Their leaders are kings in a kingdom of beggars, profiting from the misery of their subjects but making no effort to lift them out of it. That is why we lean to the extreme Left and the reactionary Right, while the party which calls itself Christian and Democratic has tried to create a confessional state, neither Christian nor Democratic. We demand to be led, no matter where, because we lack the courage to walk a man's road, even if it means walking alone."

I agreed with the old man. His thought was the thought on which is founded the best in our own way of life. But, I asked him, given the situation as it exists, given the state of mind as it exists, how do you make a start? Where is the fulcrum on which to rest the lever of reform? I returned to the story of my journalist friends, to their fear of unemployment and of prison.

The old scholar snorted angrily.

"Then let them lose their jobs! Let them go to prison! That was one thing Mussolini and the Fascists taught us—how to go to prison, how to starve for the things we believed. There is your fulcrum. There is no other. It is one man's courage and strong heart. The courage of many is what makes a good life for all."

This, too, was true, but I wanted more yet. I pointed out that he knew—none better—that the growth of truth and courage and their flowering to common effort was a slow process. I pointed out that he was an old man with a lifetime behind him, that his colleagues were working to disseminate the doctrine of the dignity of man and the need for co-operation and personal sacrifice, but that it might be decades before the fruit of their years was gathered.

The scugnizzi of Naples were the core of this book. They were, in every sense, a product of the ills of Italy. Their need was a symbol of a million other needs. If a solution could be found for them, it, too, could be a symbol, a rallying point for reform.

Salvemini looked at me, quizzically.

"And what is your solution, my friend?"

I gave it to him, tersely.

"Get them out! Found farm schools and trade schools for them in Australia, in America, in Canada, in Rhodesia. Ship them out as students, like the Barnardo and the Fairbridge boys from England. Then, when they are grown, they are already useful citizens of a new country. They create no problem of integration. They are no charge on the state. On the contrary, they are productive members."

"And where would the money come from?"

I told him I believed it could be raised from private charities, from Italians who had settled in these countries and made a good life, from Church organisations and citizen groups. He had seen himself how such things were done.

He nodded, soberly, and asked me another question.

"And how do you ask these people, these organisations, to do what Italians refuse to do for themselves?"

"By stating the simple truth—that these are children, and a child has claims on the hearts of all the world."

As I said it to Gaetano Salvemini, I say it now to all those who may read this book.

*   *   *

It is not enough, of course, to say what should be done. Unless a writer can offer a practical solution to the problems he poses, he had better not write about them. To do so otherwise is to make a theatre piece out of the misery of his fellows.

When I was a very green young man, I served a brief apprenticeship with William Morris Hughes, Prime Minister of Australia, and an inveterate enemy of Lloyd George and Woodrow Wilson. Clemenceau, the Frenchman, admired him and Orlando, the Italian, disliked him, probably because he was as canny a rabble-rouser as ever stalked the boards. He taught me one lesson I have always remembered.

"Rhetoric," he would say, "makes good politics and bad practice."

Billy was a black Welshman and his Celtic counsel has been much in my mind during the writing of this book.

Italy is the home of rhetoric and Naples is the fountain of sentiment. Roman oratory has seduced more than one diplomat and Southern charm has seduced a thousand visitors into love affairs with a very tawdry mistress.

So now I turn pragmatist and say in plain terms how folk in other countries can help the urchins of Naples.

On April 13th this year I wrote in identical terms to the United States Ambassador and to the Australian Minister in Rome. I chose these two countries, not because they are the only ones to which emigration is possible, but because I am the citizen of one, and because the other is so deeply involved in the affairs of Italy.

These were the terms of my letter:

... This work (the House of the Urchins) has now reached a critical phase. Don Borrelli takes these boys from the streets, educates them until the age of seventeen or eighteen years and then must send them out into the insecure and often sporadic employment of Naples where there is a constant pool of nearly 200,000 unemployed.

The best hope for these boys—and for the work itself— would be emigration to a specially organised farm-cum-technical school in Australia, America and Canada. Would Your Excellency be good enough to inform me—for publication in the closing chapters of the book—on the following points:

(1) If such a reception school were set up and maintained by private charities in Australia/America, would the present provisions of Australian/American immigration laws permit the entrance of a limited number of boys each year?

(2) If any impediments exist to such immigration, what are they and what action would be required to remove them?

On April 23rd, I received the following reply from the Australian Minister, Paul Maguire:

> There is nothing in the Immigration Act to prevent the admission of a limited number of boys each year in the circumstances described. The boys would, of course, have to satisfy the conditions of the Immigration Act and any criteria applied by the Australian Government under the Act ... Migration policy, in general, favours young migrants, but you will understand that specific projects for migration and individual migrants are treated on their own merits, as to suitability, health, etc.

In essence the reply is favourable. Stripped of its cautionary phrases and official options, it indicates that the way is open for private charity to provide a future in Australia for Borrelli's boys. The way is open, specifically, for those Italians who have found a good life to share the fruits of it with the lost children of their own country. How to do it?

There are a dozen blueprints available, but I suggest this one as the most practical and profitable to the country and to the boys themselves. Let them provide land, building and maintenance funds to set up a farm-cum-technical school in a good mixed farming area, where each year thirty or forty boys can be sent from the House of the Urchins to be trained as agriculturalists or specialist tradesmen.

If the capital outlay and the maintenance costs of such an enterprise seem too great, let them found the same number of resident scholarships in established institutions and charge themselves with the passage money, the clothing and the home life of the boys during the training period.

In point of fact, the second scheme could be used as a preparation for the first and the initial batches of boys could assist those who came later, under a system analogous to that of the British Big Brother Movement.

One could write volumes on the organisation and administration of existing schemes, but all the volumes can be boiled down to one paragraph:

The need is evident. The way is open under the law. Let men of goodwill do something about it.

The following is the text of the reply from the American Consulate General in Naples. The date is May 22nd, 1956:

> Your letter of April 13th, 1956, to the Ambassador, requesting certain information regarding the emigration to the United States of Italian boys, about 17 or 18 years of age, for possible training in a technical or agricultural school, has been referred to me for reply.
>
> Italian citizens, if qualified for immigrant visas, can obtain such visas subject to the quota limitations established by the Immigration and Nationality Act of 1952. The quota for Italy is 5,645 per annum.
>
> At the present time, the Italian quota is heavily over-subscribed. This presents the principal impediment to emigration to the United States on a larger scale. The quota could be increased only by an Act of Congress.
>
> It would not be appropriate for me to express an opinion regarding the desirability of establishing an agricultural-technical school in the United States for the purpose of training young Italian immigrants. The Federal Government of the United States does not control education in the United States, since education is a matter that falls within the jurisdiction of each of the forty-eight states.

I have no comment to make, no criticism. I am aware of the provisions of the McCarran Act. I pay no American taxes, therefore I do not presume to comment on American legislation or diplomatic practice.

I put it to the American people, as I put it to the rest of the world: These are children. What can you do for them?

CHAPTER TEN

IT WAS my last day in Naples, my last in the House of the Urchins. I had a sheaf of photographs in my suitcase and a pile of notes and figures. Tomorrow I would go back to Sorrento to put them in order and begin work on my book. Later, when the sirocco stopped blowing and the sea was calm, I would cross to the garish little island of Capri where the first guests of the season were already installed and where the dollar princess would come for her honeymoon with a musical-comedy prince.

I would turn my back on the bassi and on the grubby, hopeless children and sit under the wistaria and the fresh vine leaves and drink red wine and watch the girls go by in the bright little square of Capri. When the moon came up, I would climb to the Salto di Timberio and look out across the lucent water to the bobbing lights of the fishing boats.

I would hear music and laughter, and the voices of the urchins would fade to a tenuous puling cry, half-lost in the murmur of the Siren song.

I felt a little ashamed of myself. But a writer, too, is a sort of urchin, wandering the cities of the world, making his little mimes for the laughter or the tears of his readers.

So, when I sat for the last time in the dusty cluttered room of Don Borrelli, drinking my last cup of coffee, smoking my last cigarette, I was touched with the sadness of inevitable farewell.

Borrelli looked worn. He had had a big day. Tomorrow would be another, and the day after, and all the days of all the years ahead of him. He ran his fingers through his hair in the familiar gesture and gave me a tired grin.

"Do you think your book will help us, my friend?"

I shrugged vaguely. I told him I didn't know. I told

him that a book was rather like a child. You begot it in love, matured it with care and gave birth to it in considerable pain. Its fate depended on many things outside your control: the good judgment of your agent, the demands of magazine editors, the shape of your publisher's spring list, the mood of the critics and the reading public. I told him that I would write it with care, more than that, with love and compassion and all the talent I could muster. After that, *chi sa?* I hoped it would touch many hearts. I could not guarantee it would reach even one.

Borrelli flung out his hands in a passionate gesture.

"But they must read it, Mauro! They must understand what goes on here. They must know what happens to the children, not only to my children, but to all the others. The boys who are still on the streets, the girls who will end up there in due time. If they do not stretch out their hands to help us, we are lost."

I nodded wearily. I knew that as well as he did. I tried to explain that, often when people did not help, it was because they had their own problems—living costs, taxes, marital disputes, mortgages falling due, illness in the family.

He caught at the tag of my speech and worried it like a terrier.

"The family! That is the thing they must understand. We are all one family, all of us! We are sons and daughters of one Father—Arabs, Greeks, Indians, Chinese, even Neapolitans! If one of us is ill, the infection touches all the rest. An injustice done to one is an injustice to the whole family. What is the old proverb? 'A bear coughs at the North Pole and a man dies in Peking!' Look, Mauro . . .!" He planted the palms of his hands firmly on the desk and leaned across to me. "Twenty years ago in Europe we began to hear rumours of concentration camps and men killed in dark cellars and children beaten into betrayal. We shut our eyes and our ears. We shut our hearts, too. So there was a war. And after the war came the new terror of the atomic bomb, a terror that grows darker every day. Now it is not one nation but the whole human family that is threatened. And the threat is here—in Naples! The threat is wherever people are hungry, workless, without hope for themselves or their children."

I sat silent. What was there to say? I believed in the human family as Borrelli did. The book I hoped to write would be an affirmation of it. Borrelli's work was a stronger affirmation than mine would ever be. But, between the affirmation and the change stood a thousand obstacles, ten thousand men. Not all the obstacles were evil, not all the men were rogues. You couldn't throw open the frontiers and pack three million workless into ships and dump them, homeless and helpless, to disrupt another economy. You couldn't wave a wand and see a hundred factories spring up in Naples.

"No," said Borrelli, grimly. "But one day, soon, if we are not careful, someone will wave a wand, and there will spring up a hundred thousand armed men. It happened in China. It happened in Indo-China. It is happening now in Egypt and Morocco. Workless men become desperate men, and if we do not put tools in their hands, they may well arm themselves with guns. And what then happens to your good people with their living costs and their mortgages and their children with a toothache? They are committed now, as part of this human family. They are committed to its future as to its present. Look at this!"

He scrabbled under a pile of papers and found the day's copy of the Rome *Daily American*. He marked a page with a stub of blue pencil and thrust it under my nose.

The paragraph was a report of Attorney-General Herbert Brownell's recommendation to liberalise the McCarran-

Walter Immigration Act. It contained a quotation from Richard Arens, Counsel of the Immigration sub-committee. Arens's contention was that Brownell's proposal 'would change the cultural pattern of our immigration from northern and western Europe to southern and eastern Europe'.

I read it and handed it back without comment.

Borrelli said, quietly:

"Cultural pattern! You see? The old fabulous monster. The old, old heresy. What century do these men live in? Do they understand what they are talking about? This is what made ghettoes and concentration camps and destroyed freedom. This is what makes war today. Does a child have a culture pattern?"

I pointed out, as carefully as I could, that I was not an American citizen and therefore could not on the strength of a newspaper paragraph commit myself to a sweeping criticism of American legislation. I pointed out that newspaper quotations were apt to misplace the emphasis and distort the argument. Borrelli admitted it, grudgingly. But he was not to be turned so easily from his thesis.

"*Ebbene!* Let us admit for a moment this culture pattern. Let us admit that there must be a cost or a condition before you can put bread into a child's mouth or offer hope to a youth. In this country of America—in your country of Australia—migrants from this culture pattern of the South have made contributions to the prosperity of your countries. They have helped to develop them to the prosperity they enjoy today. By what right do you say '*Basta*! Enough! Now we want no more of you. Let us enjoy the fruits of your labour, but do not bother us with talk of children in the streets and men without work in the bassi of Naples!'"

Now it was my turn to be angry, not because I disagreed

with his argument but because my mind and my heart were full of all the things I had seen and learned about the sins of Italy itself. I rounded on him. I told him facts and figures. I gave him names and circumstances, many of which I have had, for obvious reasons, to omit from this published document. I told him that Americans and Australians had done much more than many of the signori of Naples, the industrialists and the absentee landlords. I pointed out that even our indifference was a virtue compared with the active opposition of his own Italians to any hint of social reform.

He took it well. He nodded soberly when I laid out the damning facts and the frightening figures. He did not challenge the argument. He agreed that the prime responsibility lay with those who were the closest relatives of the family, the Italians themselves. He refused to depart from his first premise that we were all of a kinship, and that if some failed in their duty the others must supply the default.

The anger was gone from him now and he grinned at me across the desk—a crooked urchin grin from the father and brother of the scugnizzi. He held out his hand.

"Write a good book, Mauro. Tell them who we are and what we are, not only the scugnizzi, but all of us here in Naples. Tell them we are not all rogues and touts and venal tourist guides. If we are shabby, it is because we are poor. If we hang our washing on the balconies it is because we have no other place to put it. If some of us are a little dirty, it is because we must walk down six flights of stairs to draw a bucket of water. We are an old people and a tired one; but we have endured a long time because we are not without courage. We are vain, like children, and like children we are easily moved to tears and to laughter and to anger. Like children we have our own innocence, that not even Naples can totally destroy. Explain us a little. Explain my boys, too. If you cannot find them a welcome in the good countries, ask your people at least to help them make a good life here. God keep you, Mauro. God keep all of us in the dark times!"

I wrung his hand and left him—a tired, faithful man, sitting alone in the pool of yellow light that flowed over his littered desk. Little Antonino was waiting to kiss me goodnight and Peppino would be coming to take me on my last tour of the city.

*　　*　　*

I climbed the narrow stairs to the little dispensary at the top of the building and found Antonino waiting for me. He perched himself on the bed and watched me solemnly while I shaved and put on a clean shirt and packed my clothes and changed the film in my camera. He didn't say very much. He just sat there, sucking a lollipop I had given him and following every movement with his wide, rolling eyes.

Only when I had stowed the last of my laundry and laid out my pyjamas on the bed, did he give any hint of his thoughts.

"*T'n' vai via stasera*, Mauro? Are you going away to-night?"

"No, Nino. Not tonight. Tonight I am going to dinner with Peppino. I am coming back here to sleep. In the morning I am going away."

"Will I see you then?"

I shook my head.

"Probably not, Nino. I'll be leaving before you are even awake."

His eyes filled up with tears. With the lollipop stuck in his jaws and the chocolate all over his face, he looked almost comically sad. But it wasn't comic to me. This weedy little urchin had come to symbolise for me all the miseries of Naples, all the injustice heaped on the unsuspecting shoulders of the children. I had come to love him. I

175

wanted to take him away with me. I had even made enquiries to see whether it could be done, but ten minutes'
acquaintance with the problems involved had convinced
me that it was impossible.

"You'll come back, Mauro?"

"Probably, Nino."

How could I tell him that I might never be back? How
could I explain that the lines of a writer's life are cast in odd
places and that he can never be sure from one year's end to
another where they are likely to lead him? I sat down on
the bed and took him on my knee. He put his arms round
my neck and kissed me, smearing chocolate all over my
freshly shaven face.

"Tell me a story, Mauro—just one before you go."

"Which story?"

"*L'Orso e l'Albero*. The Bear and the Tree."

It was my own rough translation of the story of the little
koala who lived on the leaves of a special kind of gum tree
and was so greedy that he ate himself out of house and
home. I had embellished it with sub-plots about the
kangaroo and the bright-coloured grass-parrots and
the big red galah and the wombat who burrowed in the
ground like a monstrous mole. What kind of fantasies
the child had woven out of my halting tale, I couldn't
guess. The Italian version was so full of circumlocu-
tions and laborious descriptions, that he might have been
dreaming of dinosaurs. All I know is that he enjoyed it
mightily.

So tonight I told it to him for the last time. He sat
quietly, sucking his lollipop, his eyes dilated, lost in the
fabulous legend of a land he might never see, a land where
nobody was hungry.

Some day, I hoped, the charity of private citizens and the
wisdom of statesmen might make it possible for Nino to

enter this land, to be educated there, to grow tall and strong and stand like a free man on good green land. But the hope was a long way off and to tell him of it would be to leave him cheated again.

When I had finished my story, I kissed him quickly, shoved another lollipop into his hands and hustled him off to the dormitory. I could not bear to have him there and to feel so empty of hope for him. He was a child, like my child. He belonged to no party. He had no culture pattern. He was a child of the streets, standing with his face pressed against the iron bars of somebody else's garden. I wondered if there were kindness enough in the house to open the gates and let him play awhile among the flower-beds.

* * *

I was worried about my dinner date with Peppino. I had suggested it on an impulse, thinking to gratify him with an evening out in a good restaurant after all our nights of tramping the back streets and the hovels. He had hesitated a moment, then accepted with warmth and enthusiasm. Only later had I realised that he might not have clothes to wear to a well-dressed place. I feared he might have committed some extravagance to get them.

He had. He had hunted all over Naples for a new jacket with a price tag to fit his pocket book. Finally, he had found it—a snappy blue model with brass buttons like an English reefer jacket. This, with a haircut and a shoeshine and a dry-cleaning for his trousers, had set him back 13,000 lire—half of his life's savings. When he came to meet me in the gardens of the Villa Communale, he was as spruce as a tailor's model.

I whistled my approval and he strutted up to me with a broad grin.

"You like it, Mauro?"

"*Bello!*" I patted the shoulders. "*Bellissimo!*" I spun him round and admired the short, tight cut and the nipped-in waist.

"The latest style, *non è vero?*"

"Certainly the latest style!"

"And the cloth?" He made me finger the lapel and feel the rayon lining of the sleeve. "The best quality?"

"The very best. You have good taste, Peppino."

He was absurdly pleased at the compliment and he suggested that as this was the hour of the passeggiata, we should walk a little and show ourselves off before we went to dinner. Fine! We would walk awhile.

The wind had dropped. The air was still and warm with the promise of the soft cleansing rain. After my long nights in the bassi, it seemed to me that the folk were brighter and better dressed and more animated. The girls giggled and swung their hips proudly and the swains were ardent and open in their flirtations.

Spring was coming to Naples and the people of Naples were opening their hearts and arms to greet it.

Peppino walked with head high and chest stuck out, acutely conscious of his new clothes and the fine figure he he was cutting in this fashionable promenade. He ogled the girls and criticised the looks and the dress of the males. I ribbed him about it.

"That's what you should be doing now, Peppino—looking for a girl to match your clothes."

He blushed and grinned.

"That's what I'd like to be doing, Mauro."

I gestured widely.

"Come now. Why not? The city's full of girls."

His face darkened.

"For tonight, yes. But for tomorrow and the day after tomorrow, to become fidanzato and to marry and have children? That is a long time away, Mauro. Sometimes I think it will never come."

Instantly I regretted my little joke. Our evening was getting off to a bad start. But I had opened the question. Now I was stuck to answer it. I patted his shoulder and said with more confidence than I felt:

"It'll come, Peppino. Probably sooner than you think. You'll find yourself a good job. You'll find yourself a good girl. You'll make a life for yourselves."

"There—in the bassi?" He jerked his thumb back towards the city. "Never!"

After his calm and compassionate expositions of the life of the scugnizzi, his vehemence surprised me. It should not have done. After all, spring was coming and the sap was running strongly in his wiry body. It was normal that he should feel the need of love, natural that he should resent its denial.

To divert his attention, and for want of anything better to say, I caught his arm and turned him round to face the bay, where a big passenger liner was steaming out into the dusk. Her lights were blazing and the smoke was a grey banner streaming back from the twin stacks.

She was a Britisher, homeward bound from Sydney and Colombo and Aden.

We crossed the road and leaned on the sea wall, watching her go. As we watched, I talked to Peppino about her. I told him about Colombo and the gem dealers round the port and the green hinterland with the tea plantations and the Temple of the Tooth at Kandy. I told him about Bombay and the Towers of Silence and the snake-charmers round the Gateway to India. I talked of the ships that Sheba had built when Aden was the port for gold and frankincense and myrrh, the gifts of the Three Kings.

It was a pitiful little travelogue, I confess, but he listened, enraptured as Antonino had been by my story of the koala in the gum tree. When I had finished, he turned to me, his face sombre in the dusk.

"You see how it is, Mauro? For you all this is possible because of this land in which you were born."

I grinned, wryly, and told him it wasn't as easy as all that. I, too, had to work and save and plan. If my books didn't sell well, I'd probably end up washing dishes in a London pub. He shook his head.

"It is not what I mean, Mauro, and you know it. The difference between you and me is that you *can* work and you can save and you can look forward to all these things. For us there is little work, no saving and no hope at all. The difference comes because you were born in one country and I in another. It is very simple."

Simple indeed; yet how tragically complex when you tried to change the balance and give as much justice to Peppino from Naples as to Mauro from Sydney. I gave it up. Spring was coming and it was my last night in Naples. I took Peppino's elbow and steered him towards the bright glass doors of a modern hotel on the Via Caracciolo.

It was his own choice that we should come here. When I had suggested our dinner date, he had asked awkwardly if we could come first to this hotel and drink an aperitif in the American bar. When I asked him why, he explained that when he was a scugnizzo, he used to stand outside the door and wait for the tourists to come in or out, to beg for cigarettes or earn 100 lire for carrying their bags to the bus stop. The idea of an American bar had fascinated him. He wanted to know what it looked like.

I warned him that he'd probably be disappointed. It was just a bar with rows of bottles in front of etched mirrors and chromium stools with red leather seats and a white-coated steward shaking cocktails. Fine! he told me. That was just what he wanted to see.

It was a bar like a thousand others. There was too much chromium and too much glass and too many tile pictures, and more liquor than a man could drink with a year's income. The steward had the bored look of a man who has shaken too many cocktails, and the guests were as sad or as gay as their counterparts in twenty other cities.

We hoisted ourselves on to the high stools at the bar, and the steward came in his own time to take our orders. I asked for a whisky. Peppino thought a moment, then ordered the same. The steward gave him a sidelong grin, then asked him a question in dialect.

Peppino flushed and spat out an angry reply. The steward shrugged and sidled away to his shelves.

Peppino swung round to face me. His eyes were blazing.

"You know what he said to me, Mauro?"

"What?"

"He asked me where I had picked you up and whether I expected a good profit on the night!"

I stifled a grin.

"What did you tell him?"

"I told him that you were my friend and that he was a . . ."

The word he used was pure Neapolitan. It signified a very dirty fellow indeed.

"Good for you, Peppino. Now let's forget him and enjoy the evening."

The steward brought the drinks. I paid for them. He glared when I omitted the ritual tip. When he had left us, we toasted one another and sipped a moment or two in silence, savouring the good, golden liquor which had cost a week's wages for Neapolitan workmen.

Then Peppino put it to me, so blandly that it took me unawares:

"We *are* different, aren't we, Mauro?"

"I don't know what you mean."

He nodded soberly.

"I think you do, Mauro. And I ask you to tell me the truth, because it is important to me and to many others."

I needed time to meditate on that one. To make time, I tossed the question back to Peppino.

"First, you must tell me. What makes you believe that you are different? How and in what particulars?"

Peppino jerked his thumb contemptuously at the barman.

"This, for one! You walk in here, or another from Rome or Venice—he bows and smiles and calls you Signore! For me, it is as you saw. I know I talk like a Neapolitan. I know I look like one. But that is a thing for pride, not for laughter or contempt. Perhaps it is something I do not know about? Something you can explain to me? We are friends. You need not be afraid of offending me."

And there it was again, leaning its elbows on the bar and grinning at us—the old, cockeyed dragon: culture pattern, stage of evolution, racial characteristics. His names are legion, but he himself is a very familiar monster—fear!

I ordered two more whiskies and tried to explain him to Peppino.

"The first thing you must understand, Peppino, is that we are all different, one from another. This one is tall, that one is short and round like a barrel. This one is blonde, the other is dark. Our tongues are different and our tastes in women, wine and funerals. It solves nothing to say there are no differences. There are many."

"But they are differences we cannot help or change. I

182

cannot talk like you, nor dress like you, nor even wink at the same girls. Sure, but why insult one another about it?"

"People who insult one another, Peppino, are generally ill-bred and impolite."

"No!" He was very definite about it. He laid his whisky carefully on the bar counter so that his hands would be free to expound the argument. "No, Mauro, if it were only that, it would not matter. It is not only the ill-bred and the impolite. It is all the others—the good folk, the Signori, the people who have their photographs in the papers." He leaned forward and tapped my knee. "You know what happens when the men of Naples go to the American Consulate here to ask for information about immigration. They can't get in. They crowd around outside and no one takes any notice of them. I know. I went there, myself. Is that good? Is that polite? Or does it mean that the man who sits inside is a Superior Being and we are just annoying animals."

I tried to parry the question with a smile.

"It probably means he just can't cope with so many applicants, Peppino."

"Then why not say so? Why not be orderly and polite about it? Look, Mauro! You know when somebody doesn't like you. You know when he laughs up his sleeve at your accent or your way of life. So do we."

"Sure! Sure!" It was a tale that could go on all night. I tried to take up the thread of my own argument. To state it polemically was easy enough, but to make it intelligible and personal to this dark-eyed, troubled youth, was a different matter altogether. I told him:

"There is a word in English, Peppino, which is called snobbery. It is hard to translate exactly, but it means that a man who has a large house looks down his nose at the man who lives in a little one. It means that if you come from a signorial family, you must be better than the workman who lives in the bassi. It means that a woman who dresses finely and wears expensive clothes despises the maid who helps her make her toilette."

Peppino nodded. This he could understand. It was a matter of daily experience with him.

"This snobbery is a folly, for it says that one man is better than another because of what he has, not because of what he is. It makes his merit consist in an accident of birth or of fortune, not in the warmth of his heart, the strength of his intellect, the skill of his hands. It is a folly, but a dangerous folly. Because it is based on fear!"

Peppino looked puzzled. The thought was new to him. The signori afraid of a scugnizzo! This he could not see.

"Nonetheless, it is true, Peppino. It is true of individuals, of classes and of nations. If I am rich, it does not please me to be reminded that there are children sleeping in gutters. It makes me uncomfortable. It turns my wine sour. It spoils my rest. If I have good manners and polite friends, it irks me to associate with those who tear bread apart with their hands and make gurgling noises with their soup. If I have two bathrooms, I had rather not know that there are thousands who have not running water. I am insecure in my possession, I am unsure of my right to it, I begin to be afraid. Because I am afraid, I am haughty, tyrannical, opposed to education and reform. Fear makes people selfish. Selfishness breeds jealousy and hate and suspicion. Wars are made by these things. Revolutions are made of them, too."

Peppino's next question was shrewdly barbed.

"Is that why it is difficult to enter another country—because we make gurgling noises with our soup?"

"To a point, yes. There are those who are afraid that to

184

bring in too many people from the South, will be to make a new Naples in their own country. It has happened before. It can happen again."

"If we were better educated and had better manners and were better artisans, we would be more welcome?"

"Yes."

"*Allora!*" He flung out his hands in a despairing gesture and his whisky glass shattered on the floor. The steward sneered and the other guests looked up in startled annoyance. "So, we are back to the beginning. We *are* different, so different that other folk are not happy to associate with us. To change, we need education. You know yourself, we cannot get it here. We cannot go abroad to get it. So, we stay, without hope!"

And there it was, the harsh dilemma of the South, the bitter tragedy of its simple, ignorant people.

Their own country offers them nothing. The doors of other countries open slowly or not at all.

They are children of the sun, yet they live in the darkness of the bassi. They have the fire of Vesuvius in their blood, but it smoulders dully and the smoke is scarcely seen. They are the inheritors of three thousand years of history, yet they live in the vacuum of Europe, in the place where progress stands still. They exist in a time which is no time, only a breathless syncope in the centuries.

* * *

We walked out of the American bar, struck back again to the Villa Comunale and then turned up-town to the Via Roma. Our destination was the restaurant called, 'The Three Doves'.

The lights were bright and the food was good and we drank a rich, red Barolo from the vineyards of the North. Because Peppino was a Neapolitan, his sadness didn't last long; so we were able to relax and laugh and sing when the fiddlers came in to make music for us.

By common consent, we talked no more of problems or politics or the blind alleys of economics. We were a pair of friends out on the town. Each of us offered his own store of anecdote and experience for the leisurely exchanges of the dinner table.

We ate slowly through antipasto, fish—the bright, red scorfano of the outer gulf, chicken *alla cacciatora*—the plumpest I had seen in weeks, new pears from Sicily and raisins wrapped in orange leaves. When the first bottle of Barolo was finished, we ordered another, as good friends should on big occasions like births and marriage eves.

By the time we had reached the coffee and the Stregas, the rest of the diners had gone and the waiters were clearing away the wreckage of the tables. The fiddlers had left long since, but we sat there in the hazy brightness, chewing the cud of our thoughts and remembering that this would be my last night in Naples, our last evening in one another's company.

We were full of food and wine and agreeable sentiment. Peppino was sure my book would sell a million copies and I was sure the next twelve months would see him and the senior boys riding the boundaries in Queensland or steaming past the Statue of Liberty.

We didn't believe it, either of us. We were building our little castle of illusions to take our minds off the realities that waited, twenty yards away from the glass doors of the restaurant of 'The Three Doves'.

Suddenly Peppino looked up at me, half-smiling, half-shamefaced:

"You know what I should like to do now, Mauro?"

"What?"

186

"I should like to drink another Strega and another. Then I should like to use the telephone there and arrange for a girl to attend me in the big house of appointment on the Vomero."

I knew how he felt. I felt it myself. But I had a home to go to and a love to welcome me back. Nonetheless I asked him:

"Why?"

"Why, Mauro? Because I am lonely and afraid. Because life is long and for me, as for so many others, there is so little hope in it. A man must forget sometimes. Do you blame me?"

I had too little faith in my own courage to blame him for anything. He was lonely. Naples is a lonely, brutal city. He was afraid—of the blank future and the loveless nights. Blame him? Not I.

I pointed at the rows of bottles round the wall and then at the telephone. I took the wallet out of my pocket and laid it on the table between us.

"There's all the Strega you want. There's the telephone. There is money in the wallet. What now?"

He looked at me oddly. Then he grinned and pushed the wallet back to me. He asked quizzically:

"And tomorrow, Mauro?"

I shrugged and grinned and refused the challenge.

"Tomorrow is your affair, not mine."

He nodded soberly. He looked down at his hands, then back at me. After a moment, he spoke:

"Then, Mauro, let me tell you about my tomorrow. I will wake and feel ashamed of myself and know that I am less a man than I want to be, and that I am two steps nearer the street from which I came."

"And so?"

The light was golden on the Strega bottles and the wallet

still lay on the table between us. Peppino pushed back his chair.

"So, Mauro, you will walk back with me to the House of the Urchins and we will say goodnight and goodbye, and when you write your book, you will say that I was your friend, *Va meglio così, non è vero?*"

I nodded, not trusting myself to speak.

It was better this way, as he said. Better for him, better for me. Better for all the world to know how love could pluck a boy from the gutter and make him more a man than many who have slept in white sheets every night of their lives.

We stood up together. I paid the bill and together we walked into the moon-bright, moon-cold city, settling now to sleep in the stink of its ancient sins.

ENVOI

Now I am come to the end of my book, which is the book of the Urchins of Naples.

I have written it with love, with indignation, and often with terror.

I have written it for the children who have no voice, for the dead who are voiceless, too.

Good, bad or indifferent, it is one man's tilt at indifference, injustice and the evil done to the children. It is one man's homage to the good he has found, and the men in whom it is personified.

If it dies unread, so be it. But let it die from lack of talent in the writer, not from lack of love in the human family, nor from want of belief in the fatherhood of God and the brotherhood of Man.

CHILDREN OF THE SUN
TWO LETTERS

Publisher's Note:

In this edition of *Children of the Sun* we are printing two letters about the work still being done in Naples and England for 'The House of the Urchins'. The first comes from the Roman Catholic Archbishop of Westminster who has visited Father Borrelli, and the second from the Dean of Westminster. Readers wishing to help the fund, may send contributions to The House of the Urchins Fund, Midland Bank, 69 Pall Mall, London, S.W.1.

HOUSE OF THE URCHINS,

NAPLES.

Spring, 1961

When I first read *Children of the Sun* I was very sceptical. Travellers' tales usually leave me unimpressed. The reports of journalists—especially those who are also novelists—have to be received with the greatest caution. So I wondered how much of this story was true. If the facts are as alleged it is obvious that the work of Father Borrelli deserves every support. But how much is fact and how much is imagination?

I decided to investigate. That is what I am doing now in the House of Urchins. Called to Rome by the Pope to take part in the work of the Secretariat for Fostering Christian Unity, I have slipped away from the Eternal City to see for myself what is going on here in Naples. The House of Urchins is a poverty-stricken patched-up ruin of a building. That, you would think, is deplorable. But no. That, according to Father Borrelli, is exactly as it should be. These boys are not in a showcase. They are not in a Home. They are at home. Home to them used to mean the streets. It still means the streets—plus a rough shelter and abundant affection. It is the combination which works wonders for these little fellows. They would not feel at home in a streamlined house. If this disused church were too clean, they would feel strangers and dirty.

Earlier today I went to Materdei, a second broken-down house in which Father Borrelli has the smallest urchins. As I was walking across the yard—no easy task with forty fingers poking to see if you are real; and twenty tongues asking how much you paid for your pectoral cross; and how much your ring is worth—I saw one undersized boy of seven rush at Father Borrelli and hug his leg: *"Tu sei mio padre,"* "You are my father," the little boy said with a look partly of love and partly of appeal.

It was the appeal that made me wonder. There was nothing strange about anyone loving this priest. I made it my business to find out the reason for that look of appeal. The child, like the rest, had never known parental love. He arrived only a few days ago and he can't believe his good fortune in having someone who really cares about him. The unspoken appeal is to be allowed to remain. Never again does he want to be starved of love.

Wouldn't it be better, I wondered, to have this place made really smart? No, said Father Borrelli, that would be a very bad thing. As soon as you build a smart house you become an institution. That is one thing which must never be allowed to happen. An institution must have rules. People who live there become inmates. They are bound to be regimented. Children in an institution do not yawn, stretch themselves and say, "Well, I'm for bed." They are for bed when the bell rings. Then they are assembled for night prayers and marched in silence to a dormitory. That must never happen to the Borrelli children.

In the House of Urchins boys behave as any boys do at home. Sometimes they are good, sometimes bad. Sometimes they love each other, sometimes they fight. There are no more rules here than in any family. Certainly no written rules for a boy to study if he wants to be kept here. Boys here do what boys do at home. They don't draw on walls and smash windows. When they go out to play they usually remember to come back in time for their meals. The big boys go and come as they please. Little boys are given the same supervision as good parents give to little boys anywhere.

Most people have heard the expression "See Naples and die". For Father Borrelli this has a double meaning. Many a child, because he first saw the light in Naples, did, in fact, die. Naples is a city of startling contrasts. The beauty of the bay, the misery of the slums. The enterprise making the Naples coastline a panorama of luxury flats, thousands living in a squalor too degrading to describe.

If you have seen how the very poor in England keep chickens you have some idea of how the poor in Naples keep themselves. In English backyards you may see makeshift hen-houses of boards, pieces of tin and old twisted wire. The filthy white hens and the sordid chicken-run depress you. Go to Naples and see how thousands of men, women and children are living. Our English slums by comparison are palaces. I beg you to believe that I do not exaggerate.

From all this horror Father Borrelli has saved a few hundred boys. His own work will expand and others will learn by his example. He may even succeed in creating a social conscience among the leaders of his city. We have much to do at home before we can be satisfied that social justice is being observed. But at least it is not being affronted as it is in Naples.

May God bless Father Borrelli and all who help him to extend his compassionate work.

✠ JOHN C. HEENAN
Archbishop of Westminster

THE DEANERY,

WESTMINSTER.

A crying human need has evoked, in Father Borrelli, a deeply human answer.

In such a man and such a priest the Church shows itself to be a flexible spiritual organism, addressing itself to one human crisis in the contemporary situation and in a way which kindles the imagination of those who have never seen Naples or the House of the Urchins.

Once the imagination is kindled, the heart follows, and people of every Christian allegiance find themselves drawn together by the magnetic attraction of a man they have never seen, working among children whom they will never know, in a place whose need until now has never impinged upon their consciousness. Such can be the effect of the special vocation of a priest in

Italy upon Christians in the British Isles. Human need is one, the world over, and Love is One, the world over. The need cries out and Love provides the man.

I for one feel privileged to be associated with Father Borrelli and his enterprise, and in commending this new edition of *Children of the Sun* I am confident that he and his boys will quite spontaneously under-cut our Christian divisions and will make through this book many hundreds of new friends and supporters.

ERIC ABBOTT

For Australian and Canadian readers:

The names and addresses of the Organizing Secretaries on the House of the Urchins Fund Australian Committee are:

> Mrs Gerda Pitsch, P.O. Box 15, Killara, Sydney, New South Wales.
> Mrs G. Leeman, c/o Treyvaud & Co., 470 Bourke Street, Melbourne, Victoria.

The name and address of the Organizing Secretary of the House of the Urchins Fund of Canada is:

> Miss Phyllis N. Lee, 45 Alexander Street, Ottawa 2, Ontario, Canada.